Boosting Your Child's Natural Creativity

Susan Daniels, Ph.D. and Daniel B. Peters, Ph.D.

Edited by: William D. Beuscher
Editorial Assistant: Donna Drake
Interior design: The Printed Page
Cover design: Kelly Crimi
Illustrations: Asher Browne

Published by
Gifted Unlimited, LLC
12340 U.S. Highway 42, No. 453
Goshen, KY 40026
www.giftedunlimitedllc.com

© 2022 by Susan Daniels and Daniel B. Peters

ISBN: 978-1-953360-11-3

All rights reserved under International and Pan-American Copyright Conventions. Unless otherwise noted, no part of this book may be reproduced, stored in a retrieval system, or transmitted in any form or by any means—electronic, mechanical, photocopying, or otherwise—without express written permission of the publisher, except for brief quotations or critical reviews.

Gifted Unlimited and associated logos are trademarks and/or registered trademarks of Gifted Unlimited.

At the time of this book's publication, all facts and figures cited are the most current available. All telephone numbers, addresses, and website URLs are accurate and active; all publications, organizations, websites, and other resources exist as described in this book; and all have been verified as of the time this book went to press. The author(s) and Gifted Unlimited make no warranty or guarantee concerning the information and materials given out by organizations or content found at websites, and we are not responsible for any changes that occur after this book's publication. If you find an error or believe that a resource listed here is not as described, please contact Gifted Unlimited.

PRAISE FOR BOOSTING YOUR CHILD'S NATURAL CREATIVITY

Parents and educators alike will find this volume a welcome companion! Daniels and Peters offer a magnitude of relevant, easy to implement strategies for those seeking to instill creativity in their children or students. Ultimately the children themselves benefit from this work which is based in research and decades of experience. Perhaps most importantly, the recommendations offered are joyful to implement and not only strengthen skills, but also deepen relationships. Well done, Drs. Daniels and Peters! This text itself is a gift.

—Dr. Norma Hafenstein, Daniel L. Ritchie Endowed Chair in Gifted Education, University of Denver

Boosting Your Child's Natural Creativity is an exquisite guide for parents, caretakers and educators to naturally nurture a creative mind, filled with easy tools and exercises for boosting everyday creativity and developing a mastery of your child's creative gifts. Drs. Daniels and Peters share their collective expertise of creativity with an innovative and compassionate approach, where you will be empowered to boost your child's natural creativity and may even find your creative spark along the way!

—Nicole A. Tetreault, Ph.D., author of *Insight into a Bright Mind*

"Art washes away from the soul the dust of everyday life," so said Pablo Picasso. *Boosting Your Child's Natural Creativity* teaches us that creativity is a vehicle toward unfettered joy. Drs. Dan Peters and Susan Daniels provide a perspective of creativity that includes everyone from the artist to the thinker, the athlete to the tinkerer. Using anecdotes of uninhibited, wildly clever children, Dan and Susan remind us of the authentic, inherent creativity we all have – perhaps latent, but always abundant – within ourselves. By showing us pitfalls that discourage creativity they help us find opportunities to engage our children in imaginative thinking in everyday ways. If you're interested in learning about, finding, encouraging, and boosting your child's relationship to the process of expressing imagination, if you'd like to light up your brain and feel flow, this book is for you.

—Julie Skolnick, M.A., J.D., Founder, With Understanding Comes Calm, LLC, Let's Talk 2e and 2eResources.com

Daniels and Peters have put together the quintessential guide to understanding and developing creativity as a means of enhancing one's lived experience. They have successfully argued the case that creative endeavor is essential to developing the positive mindset needed to navigate life's challenges. A combination of theory, practical strategies, and real-life accounts, *Boosting Your Child's Natural Creativity* covers everything you need to know about the importance of implementing creative expression on a daily basis. I wholeheartedly endorse this important work.

—Mike Postma, Ed.D., Programming Director,
Supporting the Emotional Needs of the Gifted

Dedication

From Susan:
For April, Devin, and Adeline

From Dan:
For Lizzie, Sadie, Joe, and Tobie

Contents

Introduction

When we wrote the first version of this book in 2012 (then titled *Raising Creative Kids*) we started by saying, "These days, life seems to be getting more complex, and so do our children." And now while writing this updated and expanded version—*Boosting Your Child's Natural Creativity*—in 2021, we are in the midst of a pandemic with work and school being predominately virtual. It is safe to say that life is more complex, as is raising children in this age of uncertainty and change. As educators and psychologists, we continue to be struck by the increase in highly creative, divergent thinking, intense, and sensitive children we see. Similarly (and not coincidentally), the need for parental guidance seems to be increasing, as traditional parenting approaches haven't shown themselves to be very effective in helping raise "compliant" and "successful" children, much less creative, imaginative, and innovative ones. As parents ourselves, we have a personal understanding of the challenges that parents of creative children face in today's world—both for those children's present and for the future in which they are going to live, which is constantly changing.

Many of our courses, counseling sessions, enrichment programs, and summer camp sessions have led to some common questions from parents of creative children: "Where can I learn more about how to support my child?" "How can I nurture my child's creativity when he's not getting that at school?" "Are all kids so intense and driven?" "How do I respect my child's individuality while also helping her adjust to necessary rules in life?" "Why is my child able to focus on things he is interested in but not on the things he's supposed to do?"

Do any of these questions sound familiar? Do they resonate with you? They certainly fit with our parenting experiences.

We give talks, training sessions, and presentations about these topics and issues, but we realized that we were not able to locate any single source for the useful information, ideas, and strategies for nurturing, supporting, and *boosting* children's natural creativity that parents continued to ask for. There are several books available that offer useful information about the different elements of creativity in children, but we want to bring this information together in a single volume.

Boosting Your Child's Natural Creativity is a book for parents who know that their child has creative potential and who strive to create enriched learning experiences and flexible parenting approaches to support that creativity. We are not talking about simple, time-limited approaches to enhancing creativity by sending the child away to engineering camp for eight weeks, for instance (although that sounds fun); instead, we are talking about mindful parenting approaches that are based on understanding what creativity is (and isn't), the characteristics of creativity in children, and how to parent—and teach—to help children reach their fullest creative and life potential.

Raising a creative child in modern times is an adventure. While there is no one roadmap that will work for the complex variety of children out there, we give you this book to provide the information, tools, insights, and knowledge that can *help you* in *helping your child* develop creatively and become all that he or she might be. We hope that our experiences as parents—raising creative children—and as educators and psychologists will help you on your parenting journey.

~ Susan and Dan

Chapter 1
Creativity Is for Everyone!

Everyone has creative potential! Yes, that's right. We are all born with the innate capacity for creative activity. Just think of young children ages two to five. They explore, question, wonder, experiment, test, investigate, combine, separate, enlarge, dramatize, invent, try out, try on, play, imagine, visualize, dream, adapt, build, embellish, exaggerate, innovate, transform, personify, craft, construct, pretend, improvise, revise, discover, express, decorate, elaborate, renovate, remodel, renew—and more—each and every day. Children approach their world as young inventors, explorers, engineers, architects, artists, musicians, dancers, and actors. They use the skills and habits of scientists and artists in their play, and their play is their work. Young children are naturally creative.

Yet by the fourth grade, their creative outlook often dwindles. Some children begin tearing up their papers, saying, "It's just not right!" A number of them stop taking appropriate risks and ask with ever-increasing frequency, "Teacher, is this right?" or "Mom, does this look good?"

So what happens? Well, in part, school teaches conformity, which is theoretically necessary, but which also comes at a price. Young children must learn rules for safety and for appropriate behavior in school. Certain content and skills must be learned at each grade level and then assessed for mastery. Exploration gives way to memorization and getting the right answer on a variety of quizzes and tests. Research clearly shows that creativity *can* be taught and can be nurtured, yet in the majority of today's schools, it isn't (Kaufman, J., 2010). As students progress through the grades, learning is directed more and more toward *convergent thinking*—which is essential to academic success—and less and less toward *divergent thinking*, which is essential to creativity.

Please understand: Both authors of this book are devoted to excellence in education. Learning academic content (using more convergent thinking) is unquestionably important for students, both in school and out, yet we strongly believe that academic learning should not come at the expense of developing creative potential (using divergent thinking).

Most parents and teachers believe that creativity, science, and the arts should be an important part of the school day. But the arts have been struggling to hold their place in the curriculum for some years now, science is rarely taught until middle school, and creativity has all but vanished. Mandatory standardized testing of math and reading progress has put enormous pressure on schools to demonstrate proficiency in these areas and has resulted in an increased emphasis on these two core subjects, with less time available for other areas such as the arts.

It is ironic that at the same time, numerous researchers and writers in the education field have made a clarion call for creativity to make a return as a rightful and valued aspect of teaching and learning. The 21st century has been heralded as the age of innovation. Creativity, innovation, and ingenuity are essential to solving many of the challenges facing the world today. The same old solutions that have been used for decades will not be the solutions that solve the problems of the future. Daniel Pink, in *A Whole New Mind*, argues that any activity that does not involve creativity will someday be automated and that most jobs in the future will require a high level of creative thinking.

So here we have a conundrum. Creativity is largely absent from school curriculum, yet creativity is very much needed in the 21st century.

Well, you may ask, what can we do? If you are a parent, the answer is: plenty. Parents are enormously important for nurturing, ***boosting***, and sustaining their children's natural curiosity and corresponding creativity.

Families that value creativity naturally nurture—and boost—their children's creative development. You are probably a person who values creativity; after all, you are reading this book. Being consciously aware of creativity is an important and particularly powerful characteristic of creative people. Beyond awareness, actively seeking opportunities to explore, understand, and practice creative behaviors will encourage and boost creativity in your child across his or her lifespan. You'll find this book full of ideas for developing and boosting creative potential.

Enhancing Our Understanding of Creativity Enhances Our Own Creativity

Creativity is both a capacity we are born with and a skill that we can further develop. We have been involved in the study of creativity, working with it and continually learning more about it—in ourselves, our children, our clients, and our students—for more than 50 years between us, and we are still learning. We want to share what we've learned on our journey and support you on *your* journey of parenting and teaching creative potential.

Jonathan Plucker a colleague and fellow creativity researcher, emphasizes that to approach and embrace creativity we often need to work through preconceived notions about what it is and what it isn't– as well as the question of whether we have it or we don't. He says that there are many myths and stereotypes about creativity, the most common being: *I don't have any of that.* Yet he believes that creativity is applicable to all aspects of human life.

If we define creativity as *the production of original useful things*, creativity spans an amazing breadth of activities, ideas, and products that can be called useful—from inventions, recipes, books, and songs to solutions to math problems. Creativity encompasses preferences for the unique and imaginative in people, as well as creative thought processes, creative products, and aspects of the environment that support or squelch creativity.

The Four P's of Creativity

Creativity has a long history of being discussed in terms of what are called the Four Ps of Creativity (Davis, 2004). These consist of: (1) the creative *person*—the unique characteristics that contribute to a creative outlook and a creative personality, (2) creative *processes*—the thinking skills, cognitive processes, methods of various fields and disciplines, techniques, etc. that contribute to creative ideas and products, (3) creative *products*—ideas, performances, or tangibles that are both novel and purposeful, and (4) what is called the creative *press*. "Press" in this context refers to the influence of the environment. In what ways does the environment support, shape, or suppress creativity? Is there a creative atmosphere at home or at school? Is there a Creative Zone or a particular space devoted to creative activity?

We will look at the Four P's of Creativity throughout this book from the perspective of how they may be nurtured and boosted on an everyday basis in order to support continued development of creative potential, beginning with the personality characteristics often associated with creativity. Another model of creative development, the Four C Model, helps put personality characteristics and qualities related to creativity in perspective—from the everyday creativity of designing a card for a friend to the eminent creativity of the likes of Einstein, Picasso, Curie, and Kahlo.

The Four C Model of Creativity

Before we discuss specific personality characteristics associated with creativity, we need to consider a broader conception of creativity that will frame our conviction that "Everyone is creative!" That statement is behind the notion of everyday creativity, a concept explained and supported in a book titled *Everyday Creativity*, edited by Ruth Richards (2007). Everyday creativity is the little stuff we do every day to solve problems, for example, or engage in artistic hobbies.

However, when we talk about creativity, some people immediately think in terms of eminent creators in various domains, like Albert Einstein, Frida Kahlo, Marie Curie, Maya Angelou, Thomas Edison, Langston Hughes, Twyla Tharp, and others. These well-known people are those whose ideas, discoveries, and products changed their fields forever and whose contributions we continue to respect over time, usually well beyond their lifetimes. When we think of creativity at this level only, it is easy to understand why some adults say, "Oh, I am not very creative," or even more strongly, "I don't have a creative bone in my body!"

Over the past decade—or so, researchers, scholars, and practitioners have been looking at four types of creativity, which are referred to as the Four C Model of Creativity (Kaufman & Beghetto, 2009). The four C's consist of: (1) mini-c, (2) little-c, (3) Pro-c, and (4) Big-C levels of creativity.

The Four C Model is notable for introducing and valuing *mini-c* creativity, which is a personal experience of "everyday" creativity. Examples of everyday creativity include—making a card to put in your child's lunchbox, rearranging fresh flowers for your table, building a birdhouse from scraps of wood, or putting together a scrapbook of photographs and mementos from a recent trip. We can boost creativity in small ways each day by choosing creative activities.

Little-c creativity refers to everyday problem solving and creative expression that may be linked to hobbies, avocations, careers, or extracurricular pursuits—activities that are a bit more public and receive input, feedback, and response from others—for example, quilting, painting, music performance, cooking, or decorating.

❍ What do you love to do?

❍ What does your child love to do?

- What are the creative activities that you and your child might choose to do more often? Perhaps, everyday?

Pro-c creativity refers to professional-level creativity and is exhibited by people who are professionally or vocationally creative at a higher level than the hobby level in the little-c examples but who are not eminently creative. Examples include musicians and dancers who perform as a career, as well as architects and interior designers who use art and design for their work.

Finally, *Big-C* creativity describes those who are considered truly great in their field and whose accomplishments have had lasting impact on culture and in their discipline. Examples of those who have demonstrated Big-C creativity include Mozart, Picasso, Leonardo da Vinci, Georgia O'Keefe, Frank Lloyd Wright, Marie Curie, Thomas Edison, Jonas Salk, Maya Angelou, Sigmund Freud, Julia Child, and J.K. Rowling.

The Four C Model helps distinguish between the different kinds of creativity: first, an individual's everyday participation in mini-c creative activities; second, the little-c creativity of someone who pursues creativity publicly within a particular domain (e.g., visual arts, robotics, invention, dance, etc.) in coursework or through hobbies or avocations; third, the adult professional who works creatively in a domain (software developer, artist, architect, designer, inventor, scientist) and whose work is recognized as creative; and fourth, the creative genius. The Four C Model also provides a useful framework for analyzing creative processes in individuals, and that's where we come to considering the personality characteristics associated with creativity and the mini-c and little-c potential of our children.

Table 1.1. The Four C Model of Creativity: An Overview

Level of Creativity	Qualities	Activities
mini-c	Spontaneous, private, local	A card for a friend, making a floral arrangement
little-c	Planned, deliberate, usually involves a public dimension and/or feedback from others	Designing an experiment, composing a dance performance, constructing a public exhibit

Level of Creativity	**Qualities**	**Activities**
Pro-c	Creative activity as part of an individual's professional career	Creating new aircraft designs, playing in a jazz band, city planning
Big-C	Eminent creativity, beyond professional, field-changing, surviving for centuries or more	An activity that creates a paradigmatic shift in a field or fields (da Vinci, Einstein, O'Keefe, etc.)

These four types of creativity may be considered as levels, although one does not necessarily need to progress from one level to the next and then the next. For instance, Einstein did not, as far as we know, create much as a child. He worked hard, and his imagination activated high-level creativity after years of study. Some consider mini-c creativity the domain of young children, and yet that need not be the case. Mini-c and little-c creativity may maintain and sustain creative enrichment for both children and adults. Only a small percentage of individuals will work creatively in a career as adults, and an even smaller percentage will attain eminent or Big-C creativity.

Creative Kids We'd Like to Introduce to You

As we've said—and we deeply believe—all children have creative potential. And some children are brimming with imagination and creativity. We'd like to introduce you to a few of the wonderfully creative young people we've been fortunate to meet through our work.

> *Eight-year-old Aiko is a whirling dervish, and her parents are tired. Aiko never napped as a baby. She has actively fought going to sleep every night from babyhood to the present. When asked what they remember most about her childhood, both parents spoke about her intense energy and curiosity. Her father said she was always into things. Her mother said she started talking at about eight months and hasn't stopped since. By age two, Aiko was driven to put pencil to paper. She would ignore new toys if there happened to be a pencil or crayons available to draw or "write" with. Of course, Aiko didn't actually write at that age, but she would take whatever writing implement*

was nearest, make a series of marks across her paper, and then "read" her story to anyone who would listen.

Despite her precocity, Aiko is not advanced academically. In fact, she is often bored and distracted in school and regularly forgets to finish or turn in her homework. However, when she has the opportunity to write or draw, she becomes totally engrossed and loses all track of time. She regularly makes small, illustrated books for her teachers and parents and, if asked, will happily recite or act out her stories from memory.

Aiko began showing her mini-c moments very early, scribbling, "writing," and verbally expressing her ideas. As she makes books for her teachers and parents, she is beginning to engage in little-c expressions of creativity. Will she continue on the road of creativity to Pro-c and become a professional writer? It will be interesting to watch and see.

Christian is a collector. His room has one whole wall filled with large, plastic bins—the kind you get at a discount store—loaded with "stuff." He has collected nuts and bolts, a wide variety of insulated wires, cardboard tubing of various shapes and sizes, boxes and other containers, pulleys, string and cord, hinges, random dominoes, and more. With regularity, he sets himself a new goal for an addition to "Christian's Collection of Contraptions." He has in recent months devised a mechanism to shut off his alarm clock on his dresser from a lever at his bedside, as well as a container for dispensing three different amounts of dog food to the family's three dogs. When asked why he didn't just move the alarm clock next to his bed to turn it off, he replied, "What would be the fun in that!?" Significantly, he also added, "And what would I learn from that?" Christian says he wants to be an inventor when he grows up, then quickly adds, "I'm only 10, though. I might still change my mind, you know?" Christian is considered an average student. While he has the tenacity to build complex machines that work, he lacks patience with handwriting and struggles to get his school assignments done.

Both Christian and Aiko have high creative potential. Aiko delights in creative expression throughout her day, particularly as it pertains to writing, drawing, and giving gifts of her work to others. Christian is a great example of a divergent thinker. He is constantly contemplating new ideas, new connections, and new possibilities. Further, he is playful with his approach—a sign of a creative person. At a young age, he is already thinking about using his strengths and passions as foundations for a career.

> *Sasha has had a strong community awareness since she was a young child, and she's been a member of her school's Roots & Shoots team for three years. Roots & Shoots is an enrichment program founded by the Jane Goodall Institute that requires three service projects from the teams each year; one must involve animals, one must involve people, and one must involve the environment. Last year's team took on the responsibility of replanting trees in a wilderness area that had been devastated by wildfires, an endeavor that she found particularly satisfying. Not long after that, Sasha applied for and received a small grant for researching and producing fireplace logs made from fallen leaves and a nontoxic binding agent. When asked what motivates her to work so hard on these kinds of projects, Sasha says that she likes helping people, and she really enjoys solving problems.*

Sasha is a wonderful example of a creative and compassionate person who has well-developed convergent and divergent abilities. Not only did she demonstrate her divergent thinking skills by coming up with the idea of using natural and non-toxic materials for making fireplace logs, she also was able to research her topic area, write a grant application, and meet the deadline—all convergent abilities necessary for bringing an idea to fruition.

> *Jayden's father says he was born with a question mark over his head, and his questions have since multiplied like rabbits. His mother chuckles at this comment. They both agree that Jayden's curiosity is enormous and never-ending, and his favorite phrases are "What if…?" "How come…?" "Couldn't we…?" and the ubiquitous "Why?" Both parents also feel*

as though they are walking a tightrope between nurturing their son's extensive drive to know while also teaching Jayden about respecting other people's rules and boundaries, as well as completing requirements for class assignments and group work when he is at school. When Jayden gets an idea he is committed to, he becomes a bit like a runaway train; he just keeps going and going and doesn't realize that he is seen as pushy or bossy by his peers.

Jayden is much better at thinking about possibilities than choosing the "one right answer" and therefore does surprisingly poorly on timed tests, often because he is thinking about justifications for why several of the answers might be correct. Although he is 12 years old, his parents tell us that he has kept a journal since he was roughly seven. In his journal, he draws objects—both natural and manmade—and writes notes and questions about their design and structure.

Jayden has a perpetually inquisitive mind that allows him to gain deeper understanding of the world as he searches for answers. His creative domain and product are yet to be determined. He is continually building his foundation of knowledge and his storehouse of ideas for what may come next.

Aiko, Christian, Sasha, and Jayden are just a few of the children we've had the pleasure of knowing and working with—in schools, in our center, and at our summer camp. Each young person is distinctly interesting and unique, yet they have common traits as well. They are all very curious and highly motivated; they are divergent thinkers who look at the world through a slightly different lens, seeing possibilities that others may miss; they are also driven by their own strong interests and will persist in those interests with tenacity and perseverance. Yet three of the four children we have described are not very motivated by classroom assignments or homework. In fact, they would rather not have to deal with schoolwork at all.

As you will read in this book, children who have creative strengths and characteristics that will serve them well in life—tenacity, perseverance, and problem-solving abilities—also present quite a few parenting and teaching challenges as they "march to the beat of their own drum," experience strong feelings about how they want to do things, and resist conforming to the demands of the environment, including the various tasks they are asked to complete on a daily basis. Although they are usually bright enough to be getting top grades, many creative children are not motivated in their classrooms and don't do particularly well in school. What will happen to them if they don't learn to achieve in school? What kind of future will they have?

These are valid concerns for many parents of creative children. We aim to show you that while performing in school is important, it is these children's creative personality—and your support and nurturance of that creativity—that will contribute to their being engaged in learning, creating, and producing as they become young adults, and throughout their lifetime.

Neurodivergence—Sparks of the Creative Mind and Spirit

Nicole A. Tetreault, PhD

Creativity is the burning desire at the center of your chest, the flame radiating from your core, it is the skipped heartbeat when you take a risk and the ultimate dopamine rush when in flow. Creativity is innate to your very existence and necessary for evolution. It is entwined in your DNA, part of every fiber of your being and the expression of your neuroindividuality and your essence. Pablo Picasso said, "Every child is an artist, the problem is staying an artist once you grow up."

Children are full of imagination, they have curiosity and open minds to visualize connections many cannot see. Daily acts of creativity stem from the spirit of exploration like building with Legos, baking cupcakes, solving a math equation, speaking in a mindful manner to defuse an argument, or walking home from school on an unmarked path. All activities are creative in their nature. Neurodiverse people often walk in solitude on a backtrail through life's peaks and valleys. So how do neurodiversity and creativity influence one another?

Neurodiversity arises from distinctive brain wiring and nervous system processing among the five senses (sight, taste, touch, smell, and hearing) that leads to extraordinary thinking, enhanced emotional processing, and novel behaviors and actions. Neurodivergence is found in many groups like those with autism spectrum disorder (ASD), attention deficit disorder (ADHD), dyslexia, dyscalculia, dysgraphia, dyspraxia, and giftedness. Each of these groups has diverse brain patterns that reflect novel ways to perceive and process the world. Now, creativity and originality begin with the mind, and for neurodiverse people their distinct brain wiring fuels their creativity. Frequently, neurodivergent people break away from society's confines that limit creative expression. Neurodiverse children are often challenged in traditional academic settings because they literally have different brain wiring where they see and experience the world uniquely. This can create a great deal of tension with teachers, peers and family members because neurodiverse individuals interpret, behave and speak differently from the norm. Thinking outside the box can have real consequences when a classroom prioritizes conformity over individuality. Often neurodiverse individuals are caught in their imagination and their innovation is lost in school. For neurodiverse individuals, creativity fuels their existence where they assemble connections like a constellation opening the human imagination. Edward de Bono writes, "Creativity involves breaking out of established patterns in order to look at things in a different way."

That is exactly what the neuroscience of creativity is revealing: that it is not black and white, nor is it left and right brain, it is the entire brain illuminating with energy when one is in creative flow. For each individual their brain uniquely lights up in flow. For many years, the popular myth has been that the left hemisphere of the brain is the "logical brain" and the right hemisphere of the brain is the "creative brain," but that is false. Scientists reported when individuals were engaged in creativity, three brain networks were activated that do not normally activate in synchrony, meaning the brain is lit up in technicolor when in the creative zone.[1] These three networks are the default mode network, salient network, and executive functioning network. The default mode network is active during dreaming, meditating, and daydreaming, and it is the network on in the background of all our activities. The salient network is responsible for our ability to assign the value of things and identify the emotional tone. The executive functioning network is crucial for decision making and task completion. This all makes sense, that each of these networks guide creativity because dreaming, emotions and making decisions guide the work. Understanding the neuroscience of creativity illustrates the connection between creativity and neurodiversity.

For example, studies have shown how individuals with Autism Spectrum Disorder (ASD) are inherently creative and that they come up with more novel ideas compared to peers.[2] Children with ADHD are unusual thinkers where they are very good at divergent thinking tasks with everyday objects.[3] Highly empathetic people have expanded circuitry for emotional processing and offer gifted acts of compassion.[4] Neurodiverse people often are "hardwired" to be creative.

It is important to see the value of and nurture divergent thinking. Positive talk and engagement rather than negativity and disinterest allow an individual to live in their essence and share their gifts. Nurturing is a key element to develop creativity. Stress and negativity inhibit creativity. Keeping creative spaces sacred and stress-free supports creativity. So, encourage your child in their creative pursuits by offering positive speech, emotional encouragement and deep acceptance for their unique ways of being. Creativity is inherently rewarding, so when creative people are in flow, their brain releases positive neurochemicals like dopamine, further enhancing creative expression. Creativity is good for your child's health and wellbeing. Creative expression can fuel healthy behaviors and brain patterns because children can be engrossed in their creative endeavors, experiencing life with greater purpose and meaning so that they naturally feel greater connection and more freedom to share their gifts with the world.

There is courage in creative thinking, to imagine the impossible. Be bold. Be brave. Create. Listen to the burning desire at the center of your and your child's heart and ignite the flame.

[1] Roger E. Beaty, et al. "Robust prediction of individual creative ability from brain functional connectivity." *Proceedings of the National Academy of Sciences of the United States of America* vol. 115,5 (2018): 1087-1092. doi:10.1073/pnas.1713532115

[2] Catherine Best et al., "The Relationship Between Subthreshold Autistic Traits, Ambiguous Figure Perception and Divergent Thinking," *J Autism Dev Disord* 45, no. 12 (Dec 2015), https://doi.org/10.1007/s10803-015-2518-2.

[3] White, Holly A., and Priti Shah. "Uninhibited Imaginations: Creativity in Adults with Attention-Deficit/Hyperactivity Disorder." *Personality and Individual Differences* 40, no. 6 (2006/04/01/ 2006): 1121-31. https://doi.org/https://doi.org/10.1016/j.paid.2005.11.007.http://www.sciencedirect.com/science/article/pii/S0191886905003764.

[4] Chunshui Yu, et al. "White matter tract integrity and intelligence in patients with mental retardation and healthy adults." *NeuroImage* vol. 40,4 (2008): 1533-41. doi:10.1016/j.neuroimage.2008.01.063

Boosting Creative Potential

Creative potential is a wonderful capacity to have and to nurture. Some will argue, as we shall see, that nurturing creativity is essential for life in the 21st century. Yet if we don't give conscious thought to nurturing, developing, and *boosting* creativity… creative potential may languish and dwindle.

To parent with creativity and to boost creativity in our children, we need to become more aware of the developmental aspects of creativity, the common behaviors of creativity, and strategies and approaches that encourage creative development outside of the school setting.

By definition, creativity in our children does not come in a neat one-size fits-all package. So it is essential that we get to know our children as unique individuals; that we take note of their creative potential, their creative qualities, and their creative behaviors; and that we support and nurture those qualities and behaviors so that they can be developed in the most positive ways possible. Your child is engaging in mini-c moments all the time as she expresses her ideas and individuality. You have many opportunities throughout the day to nurture and promote her creative qualities.

These are the goals we have for this book: We hope you gain some practical knowledge and strategies for stretching your own creativity while supporting your child's. We hope you discover some "ahas" (!) about your child's creative abilities and that you enjoy a good read along the way. Most of all, we hope you take away an enhanced desire to celebrate creativity and a desire to help boost your child's creative potential. We've listed a few suggestions for doing just that in Table 1.2, and many more appear in the chapters ahead. Enjoy!

Table 1.2. Celebrate Creativity—Four Strategies for Boosting Everyday Creativity!

1. *Surround yourself with creativity.* First, notice creativity; it is all around you. Then seek to enhance creativity in your life. Look for books, materials, and other people who support and celebrate creativity.

2. *Be open-minded.* Consider possibilities. Change your point of view. Look at your ideas and the world from a different perspective. Take a different route to work or to your child's school. Try a usual task in a new way. Talk about different possibilities and ideas as they come to you.

3. *Be childlike (as opposed to childish).* Play with your child as you both create. Try to see things with a child's perspective—new, interesting, and perhaps with wonder. Focus on being playful rather than serious, on being spontaneous and messy rather than neat and tidy. Try to stay in the moment with your child, rather than thinking ahead to the end and what comes next. Let your play and projects unfold naturally and avoid managing the process.

4. *Be persistent.* Make time—even a small bit, say 5 to 15 minutes each day—and make a commitment to regularly engage in mini-c creative pursuits. Keep a creativity journal. You may

want to do this while you read this book. Reflect on your creative thoughts, doodle, and daydream while keeping a record of it all. Get a sketchbook with no lines. Watch your thinking emerge in words and images.

Chapter 2
Creativity in Early and Middle Childhood: When Play Is Work and Work Is Play

Creative exploration is an integral part of growing and learning, and creativity often will permeate a child's day as he jumps from one game or dance or story or building or drawing to another and back again. A child may find her joy and a forum for creative expression in many areas, or there may be one or two areas that tend to captivate his imagination. We'll begin this chapter by looking at creativity in general as it plays out in the overall development of the infant and young child. Then we'll look at how creativity may find expression in a particular domain, such as in the case of one young man who demonstrated creative tendencies at a young age and then went on to use his creativity to earn celebrity status, or through an exploration of two or three domains, as in the unforgettable child we describe who is captivated by art, nature, and mathematics in combination.

We'd like to introduce a few more creative children we have had the pleasure to know:

> *Annika is seven years old and in second grade. She has a very active imagination. She loves animals and insists on acting like them. At recess, she likes to pretend that she is a puppy and wants her classmates to be puppies with her. At home, she has been known to curl up on a blanket on the floor, bark answers to her parents' questions, and ask them to scratch her behind her ears. Although her teacher and some of her aunts and uncles sometimes wonder if she knows the difference between fantasy and reality, Annika has told her mother, "Don't worry, Mom. I know I'm not really a puppy. It just feels so good to pretend. I love soft little puppies so much!"*
>
> *Juan is eight and a third grader. He loves Star Wars and playing with army men, setting up elaborate battles. Juan makes amazing sound effects as his characters are shooting each other and detonating bombs. He doesn't play with other children very often; he seems content playing alone for hours.*
>
> *Regan is nine and in fourth grade. She has a strong sense of fashion and has cared deeply about how she presents herself from an early age. She takes a long time to pick out her clothes and to fix her hair in the morning. Whenever she can sneak it, she experiments with her mother's makeup. Ultimately, she got her own makeup set, but only for use at home; she is not allowed to wear makeup to school or at social gatherings until she is older! Regan enjoys shopping, and her mother and older sister sometimes consult her for fashion advice. Oftentimes her various outfits bring with them a different "story" or a different persona.*

Annika, Juan, and Regan all have active imaginations. Although each one expresses his or her creativity through different mediums, all show a particular theme or interest area. While playful at the core, they all take their creative expression seriously and are committed to it, regardless of what others may think.

When a Child's Work Is a Child's Play

Every day begins a new exploration in the world of a young child. The most common experiences present themselves as opportunities for investigation and problem solving—looking deeply into the center of a flower, blowing bubbles into a glass of milk, feeling the warmth of a sunbeam on a cool day, or noticing the difference in tones produced from tapping glasses filled with varying levels of water. A child claps her hands to a beat as music unfolds and later watches oil float on a rain puddle. Each of these endeavors is both an aesthetic experience and a readymade, on-the-spot, scientific experiment, inspiring questions and hands-on exploration.

The kernel of creativity, says psychologist Theresa Amabile, is there in the infant (1989). Early in infancy, children exhibit the desire and drive to explore, to find out about things, to try things out, to experiment with different ways of handling and looking at things. As they grow older, their play becomes more complex, their experimenting more formalized, their insights and creative products more intricate. And yet, through it all, they are still essentially playing.

Adults generally play after they have finished their work. For young children, play is what they do all day; it is creating, discovering, and learning. Young children do not discern between play and work as adults do. Imagination, creativity, learning, and play are all intrinsically motivated pursuits—done for the sake of the doing. In fact, many a child psychologist has opined that children's play *is* their work (Goleman, Kaufman, & Ray, 1992).

Wired for Play, Imagination, and Creativity

Young children don't need to be taught how to play and be creative. Creativity and inventiveness are hardwired in us as a species.

Most other animal species are born with a full range of reflexes and responses already developed. Human offspring, however, have an unusually long and richly formative childhood in comparison, giving us more time to develop thinking skills and responses to the environment.

We are not born with a "completed" brain. The human brain and central nervous system continue to develop and mature throughout childhood, adolescence, and—we know now with more advanced neuroimaging—even into early adulthood. There are periods of great neuronal growth, especially around two years of age, as well as during preadolescence and adolescence. These growth periods are followed by periods of *pruning* in the brain, during which neural connections that are not used are discarded. However, those that are used with frequency form strong, lasting connections. The process of *myelination* is one in which especially strong neural pathways are insulated or reinforced so that they remain substantially robust and efficient in their connections.

From birth through young adulthood, the brain has more neurons than it will ever have again, and it is the shaping of the neural connections during this time that stimulates intellectual development, creative potential, an individual's personality, and more. A child's interactions with others, his work (and play) at school and at home, and his play within the environment will determine much of what he will know, be able to do, and become.

We'll talk about all of this again in greater detail in the next chapter. What is important to understand here is that a child's mind is a work in progress as it grows and develops. It is at this time that adults have the awesome opportunity to nourish the child's brain development, his cognitive and creative growth, and his sense of self.

Play and Creative Exploration in Young Children

As the brain develops over the course of childhood, various forms of play also develop. Toddlers are often onlookers to other children playing, or they engage in parallel play, playing next to another child but not necessarily interacting with the other child. In preschool, kindergarten, and the primary grades, children are more inclined to negotiate play together and to play with adaptable materials such as boxes and other found objects, creating worlds of their own devise. At this age, children begin engaging in imitative pretend play, in which a child might suggest, "Let's play family. I'll be the daddy," or "Let's play school," as in the case of Padma:

Padma, age six, loves to play school. She puts on her mother's high heels and old glasses and gets out her "teacher supplies," which consist of her tablet-sized white board, play clock, and class schedule. She then lines up her dolls and stuffed animals on the floor in her room, gives them each a piece of paper and pencil, and says, "Now, class, today we are going to learn math, and then there is going to be a test. Oh, don't worry; it won't be too hard. I just want you to do your best." Sometimes her "students" fall over if they are talking and being disruptive, and she has to remind them that proper classroom behavior requires staying seated and being alert at all times.

Lately, Padma has been asking her parents to be her students so that she can interact with them. She tells her father that she will plan his lesson while he is at work, and they will play school when he gets home. She says, "Be prepared to have some homework tonight." Her parents are more than willing to spend a little time each night doing their "homework" for her—creating a geometric design, a poem, or an illustration, using the detailed directions that she assigns. They are hoping that she will maintain her enthusiasm for school throughout her childhood and well beyond.

As children move toward middle childhood (roughly grades three through five), play may retain great breadth of imagination while also incorporating much more structure, as determined by the children themselves, with rules and roles and sometimes scripts, wardrobes, and even special effects. Many creative children create imaginary companions or impersonate imaginary characters. Some have entire imaginary communities or imaginary families. Some creative children develop countries, planets, and histories for their imaginary companions, including dress, language, maps, terrains, holiday customs, and more! Their explorations and stories are strongly immersive and tend to become more so over time.

Jane Piirto, writer, poet, college professor, creativity researcher, and author of the book *Understanding Creativity* (2004), found that creative children are exceptionally imaginative, have a high incidence of imaginary playmates, are prone to fantasy, and make up imaginative scenarios with their toys and with objects in the environment.

> *Evan, age eight, loves large boxes. Every box has the potential to be a fort, a house, a bomb shelter, or a secret hiding place that only he and his favorite stuffed animals can occupy. When a large package arrives, Evan's first question is, "Can I have the box?" Duct tape is good for connecting boxes, and Evan's parents supervise as he cuts holes to make doors, windows, and secret peepholes. Items like blankets, pillows, books, and a pair of toy binoculars go into the fort. When Evan is feeling generous, he lets his little sister join in the play, and they pretend to be the only people on an island or create other imaginary worlds together.*

Notice that Evan's expression of creativity is radically different from Padma's. However, both Evan and Padma are fortunate to have parents that are supportive of their creative play. Padma's mother and father are active participants in her pretend school, and Evan's parents allow him to safely build structures that sometimes take up entire rooms. These parents give up their time and their space to allow their children to express their creativity in ways that will help them grow and develop into creative adolescents and, hopefully, creative adults.

Play as Process and Product

As you can see, creativity takes many forms in young children as they play, experiment, and explore their world. Some of these children may develop a product as part of their creative activity, but many do not. This doesn't mean that those children aren't creative, however. Play is a process; it does not need to result in a product. Play may involve a single child or a group of children. It may include toys or tools or found objects, or play may be based entirely in the imagination.

No matter what form it takes, and no matter whether it produces a tangible product or not, the act of playing stimulates significant growth within a child's brain. Elaborate mental processes and mental development often result from play, including cognitive growth, growth of the child's imagination, social development, and even physical development. As adults, our greatest gift to them is to provide time and space to explore their world with uninterrupted periods of complete immersion and with opportunities to expand their understanding through their own experiments, inventions, and creations. Not only will they be happier and more creative individuals, they will be learning and growing at a critical time in their cognitive development.

Creativity Killers: When Play Is No Longer Fun

Children love to play because play is fun. It is intrinsically motivated, often spontaneous, and driven by immediate questioning, inspiration, and imagination. When adults attempt to structure play, or even interfere with play, the activity is no longer really play at all, and children's interest dwindles. Dr. Amabile, author of *Growing Up Creative,* identified five behaviors unwittingly performed by adults that kill children's creativity (1989):

1. *Surveillance*: When adults hover over children or comment or intrude on their play or creative activity, children may begin to feel that there are "right" and "wrong" ways to play, and their creative impulses and risk-taking behaviors diminish or go underground.

2. *Rewards*: Any extrinsic rewards for creative activities, such as gold stars, money, or toys switch the focus from self-motivation to the expectations of others. This hampers children's desire to create for the simple sake of fun.

3. *Over-control*: This happens when a parent or other adult tells a child exactly how to complete a project or activity or helps too much, without letting the child do it herself. Some parents become so invested in their child creating an exemplary project that they end up doing much of the work themselves in an attempt to "help" the child get a good grade or advance in a science fair. When parents take over a project, the child learns that her work isn't good enough without the assistance of an adult, and she begins to believe that her own creative ideas and efforts are inadequate.

4. *Restricting choice*: Some parents have definite ideas as to which activities their children should participate in and which ones they should not. To nourish creative development, it is much better to facilitate a child's choice based on the child's own interests and to support that inclination.

5. *Evaluation:* Dr. Amabile found that all types of evaluation—both positive and in the form of critiques—stifle children's creativity. If they know that an assessment is forthcoming, children focus too much on how their creative work is going to be evaluated rather than on their own creative immersion in the process of doing and making.

Concerning Amabile's point #5, this is not to say that adults should never comment on the work that children do. Creativity researchers James Kaufman and Ronald Beghetto have discussed what they call the "Goldilocks Principle" (2009). Feedback is certainly necessary for children, but questions arise as to what kind and how much.

- How much feedback is too much and therefore squelches intrinsic motivation?
- How much is not enough and leaves the child without any direction at all, which can be discouraging?
- How much is *just right*, encouraging the child's activity while not driving the outcome?

It seems that the answer will vary from child to child, and parents need to be keen observers to find and monitor that delicate balance. Parents can introduce feedback with inquisitive dialogue to facilitate the child's own self-reflection:

- What do you like best about your project?
- What will you do next?
- Is there anything you want to change or do differently next time?

Questions like these highlight the work-in-progress aspect of creative activity and the possibility of having another go at a project that doesn't initially turn out "just right."

True Stories of Creative Children as Artists and Scientists

We have so many stories between us of the creative children we have worked with, but rather than try to choose among them, we are going to borrow some interesting stories of creative children from others. These anecdotes help illustrate the range of content areas, topics, and expressions that creativity can take as children grow and develop. The first is taken from Goleman, Kaufman, and Ray's *The Creative Spirit* (1992), and the second is borrowed with permission from our colleague Deirdre Lovecky. It just so happens that these are stories of two Stephens.

> *It's the 1950s, and a young boy, who happens to be a Boy Scout, wants to get a merit badge in filmmaking. His father bought him a super-8 movie camera, and his mother agreed to help him with his desire to produce special effects for a horror movie. This involved a pressure cooker and several cans of cherries. These were cooked for a very long time until the oozy red goop very much resembled blood and was then used to drip from the kitchen cabinets in the critical, most creepy action shot of the movie. The gloppy bloodlike substance oozed from the crevices in and around the cabinet doors in the kitchen. Clearly, Stephen's mother was not the type of mother to say, "I don't want to deal with this. Go outside to play," even though the goopy bloody kitchen scene left her picking cherries from the cupboards for years. And it's a good thing, too, as her son, Stephen Spielberg, learned a lot from these early artistic experiments.*

Stephen Spielberg's mother was an integral component of and advocate for her son's creative process and the early development of his special effects techniques. Not every parent would set his or her child free in the kitchen with a can of cherry pie filling, nor would we ever presume to suggest that every parent should. For Stephen Spielberg, however, the process led to Big-C creative achievements.

Here's the story of the other Stephen, who is not a well-known individual. In fact, he's still a child, and we have high hopes for him.

> *Stephen, age nine, was very interested in science and math. He especially liked making things with blueprints and schematics he developed himself. Things with patterns were easy for him to learn. What is more, he was quite adept at finding the patterns within the material himself, then instantly recalling all of it once he had recalled the patterns. Stephen also loved the sea and had acquired a vast store of knowledge about sea animals, ocean currents, sailing vessels, whale migration routes, and life in the extreme depths of the deepest ocean trenches.*
>
> *In fifth grade, Stephen entered the school science fair with a project that grew from his love of the sea combined with his love of numbers. He had learned about the pattern used by the chambered nautilus in building successive parts of its shell. Stephen's project, called "Mathematics of the Chambered Nautilus," studied how this sea animal used the Fibonacci number pattern. Each turn of the spiral made by the animal is a factor of 1.618 from the center. This logarithmic spiral is also found in other aspects of nature. Stephen included information on cows, bees, and rabbits illustrating famous Fibonacci problems. He also described how many plants use Fibonacci sequences in leaf distribution, seed-head growth, and flower petal arrangement to allow for maximum packing of many elements into a small space. Not surprisingly, Stephen's project won first place at his school's science fair.*

Stephen's story illustrates the maturation of play. Can't you just see Stephen at the beach as a young boy carrying a huge shell in one hand and dragging kelp behind him? Can't you imagine him digging holes, chasing little crabs as they burrow into the sand, and collecting skeletons of washed-up sea creatures? These moments of joy, bliss, and wonder often extend to passions and focused pursuits as a child matures. We can imagine Stephen's early beach play as totally engrossing as he explored his environment. As he matured, we can imagine his sheer delight in close observation of the environment, his own scientific field study. Stephen's play was quite literally work, and yet his work is also very much play to him. What are the chances that Stephen will grow up to become a biologist?

Boosting Creative Potential Throughout Childhood

Simply put, play is a child's job. Starting in infancy, children are biologically determined to observe, explore, and interact with their environment. Early on, they develop the capacity for imagination and make believe. They start to pretend, and they love to live in the world of "what ifs." Their imaginative and creative play may or may not produce a product. If fact, that is part of what makes their play so intrinsically motivating—there does not have to be an end product that will be evaluated. They are creating and exploring for the sole purpose of creating and exploring.

As children mature, their creative pursuits become more structured and purposeful, often with products in mind, and they benefit enormously when given the space and time to create, imagine, and innovate. Creative expression often moves from mini-c to little-c as children take more initiative and interests become more defined. Older children begin seeking out creative enrichment opportunities in the way of art classes, science workshops at local museums, ideas for projects to build from online sources, team-based creative programs, and more. Over time, as children move toward adolescence, creativity emerges in the personal realm as well, as a part of their evolving identities, including style of clothing, hair color, modifications to personal space—color of the walls in the bedroom, music, posters, photos, artwork—and more.

We encourage you to enjoy and savor your young child's raw, innocent, and uncensored creative moments. Change, development, and growth are inevitable, and how you as a parent approach your child's creative play will help determine whether her creativity will be squelched or enhanced and given a boost every now and again.

Chapter 3
Personality and Creative Potential

Creativity defies a single definition or description; it is a nature and a skillset both focused and multifaceted. Yet certain qualities appear to be related to creativity in children more often than not. These qualities are found in most children to some extent, whether or not they are especially creative, until the play and imagination of early childhood give way to the strict rules and boundaries that come with standardized curriculum in schools and peer pressure to conform. Researchers have found a considerable drop in creativity and divergent thinking in children that occurs in about fourth grade (Runco, 2011). This makes it all the more important for parents and teachers to notice, encourage, and give a boost to the creative qualities present in their children—and themselves, for that matter!

Creative people tend to demonstrate or possess the following traits:

1. Open-mindedness
2. Imagination
3. Need for privacy and alone time
4. Daydreaming
5. Persistence
6. High energy
7. Independence
8. Risk taking
9. Curiosity
10. Sense of humor/playfulness
11. Attraction to complexity
12. Artistic interests and aesthetic perspectives
13. Sensitivity and intensity
14. Perception
15. Awareness of creativity

Let's look at each of these in greater detail.

Open-Mindedness

Open-mindedness is an essential aspect of creative potential. By keeping an open mind, we are able to consider new possibilities and ways of being that we have not experienced before. The ability of creative persons to be independent and to risk new ideas is at least in part due to open-mindedness. Creative individuals are open-minded as they are willing to consider possibilities and able to tolerate ambiguity while contemplating an idea. Though open-mindedness does not necessitate a complete rejection of convergence or convention, it allows people to approach what *is* as a starting point for what *might be*—a launching pad for more original explorations of what might be possible in a future context.

Open-mindedness speaks to mental flexibility. Creative people do not hold to rigid views and perspectives but are open to a variety of alternatives and solutions. They have fewer preconceived notions and are more willing and apt to generate their own ideas and solutions.

Creative children ask questions like "Why do we have to do it that way?" or "What if we do it this way?" Adults can encourage these questions, perhaps even asking them of children directly.

Imagination

Originality and imagination are part and parcel of the creative personality, as well as the creative process. Creativity often involves fantasizing, daydreaming, and other imaginative forays. Imagery also plays a key role in creative thinking and conceptualizing. In fact, creativity may involve more deliberate forms of mental imagery—that is, creative individuals have been reported to have more control over their mental images. As the eminent psychologist Jerome Singer (1999) stated, "The great human capacity for imagery, that is, reproducing mentally an object, event, or face and associated sounds, tastes, touches, or smells even after they are no longer present in one's sensory field, is an important feature of imagination."

Michael Piechowski, a leader in the field of gifted children, wrote, "Tigers might not have imagination, but imaginary tigers can be made of flames" (2006)—a novel thought, and somewhat quirky, some might say. Yet this is the way with the imagination. With imagination, anything is possible. Imagination plays a part in all creativity, from everyday creativity to the creativity of eminent individuals. When we ask, "What would I like to do today?" and subsequently think of the possibilities, our imagination is engaged. The same is true when we arrange pictures on the fireplace mantle, make chalk drawings on the sidewalk, or play jazz on a saxophone. And if one has an imagination like J.K. Rowling's, an entire dining hall with floating candelabras, wizards, and dragons can result.

Children are more often closely in touch with this capacity for fantasy and are less constrained by notions related to the finite world. In the imagination, one can travel from a stormy day in the Midwestern United States to a land where scarecrows dance, lions sing, and magic red shoes protect you. Imagination turns a sheet draped over two chairs into a fort, a castle, or a cave. Imagination gives birth to fairy tales, science fiction, poetry, plays, murals, original music, and scores of amazing inventions, gadgets, and gizmos.

We can readily nurture and support this aspect of creativity at home and at school. We can call on children's imaginations with a wealth of projects and activities. They could write an original story or play, create a fictional diary of a child from a different time or place, contemplate new designs for energy-efficient homes, or create a sculpture to represent an abstract concept. The possibilities are limitless.

Need for Privacy and Alone Time

If we want to encourage our children to actively play with their imaginations, we need to provide a few basic necessities to enable that to happen. One of those necessities is the luxury of time.

Author Graham Wallas's analysis of the creative process includes four stages (1926). They are:

- preparation,
- incubation,
- illumination,
- and verification.

Preparation is foundational; it is the stage that involves exploring, clarifying, gathering, and reviewing data; collecting resources and materials; and so on. Then next stage, incubation, is perhaps the hallmark of the Wallas model. *Incubation* is the period during which the creative activity or problem is, deliberately or incidentally, put out of one's mind. It is a time of preconscious, fringe-conscious, or unconscious processing during which one is intentionally not giving the creative project or idea attention; instead, one is involved in another activity, such as resting, reading, walking in the woods, or possibly even sleeping. It is during such periods of relaxation and reflection that the *Aha!* associated with *illumination* in the creative process occurs. Numerous creators in a variety of fields have reported a need for extended periods of solitude so that they can nurture and explore their creative ideas. *Verification* is the follow-up work that goes into testing the new idea and developing it fully for application (Wallas, 1926).

Children need opportunities for alone time. It's not uncommon for children today to be scheduled for every activity in which they could possibly participate, and while this level of participation introduces them to a variety of areas of potential interest, it also allows them very little in the way of free time. Without enough time for their brains to process thoughts and ideas, these overscheduled children lose out on the opportunity to passively engage in one of the fundamental stages of creativity. Parents should remember to include some down time in their children's schedules so that they have time to think, explore, tinker, and let ideas incubate.

Daydreaming

Imaginative children often are accused of "zoning out" or daydreaming. This tendency can be irritating to both teachers and parents alike. However, like incubation, daydreaming appears to be an important part of the creative process. While in this seemingly inattentive state, a child may be letting his thoughts float freely, but he also may be thinking intently about a particular idea or project. Adults need to be aware that a child who appears to be doing nothing may in fact be working hard—in his mind.

Just as children need free time for the incubation process, they also need down time that is unstructured and unscheduled to be with their own thoughts. They need time for contemplation, reflection, and inspiration without an adult planning, commenting on, or overseeing their activity.

Persistence

> *Nothing in the world can take the place of persistence. Talent will not; nothing is more common than unsuccessful men with talent. Genius will not; unrewarded genius is almost a proverb. Education will not; the world is full of educated derelicts. Persistence and determination alone are omnipotent. The slogan "Press On" has solved and always will solve the problems of the human race.*
>
> - Calvin Coolidge

In addition to time, persistence is a necessary trait to see the creative spark realized, to see the creative idea develop into the creative project. Unfortunately, in our highly structured classrooms and our highly scheduled lives outside of school, time is often not afforded for children to engage in creative pursuits. To nurture creativity, we must provide time for daydreaming and for reflection, as we have discussed, but also for downright relentless persistence.

Children need time to explore, to experiment, to discover, to learn from mistakes, to adjust and realign their ideas, to make corrections, to try again. These are lifetime skills that extend far beyond the measure of common academic standards. These habits of mind—and heart—will persevere well into and beyond the span of time spent in school. They are the qualities that shape a creative life. If we believe in the creative potential of our youth, then we must be willing to allocate the time necessary for the true development of their creative spirits; with time, passion, and persistence, they will flourish.

It is often hard to delineate where a passion stops and an obsession begins for creative individuals. The line can appear to blur, and it often does. To use a Big-C example, Bill Gates was known to program computers for up to 20 hours a day during college, and he spent many hours in his high school's computer lab prior to that. A child who lives and breathes everything related to cars, to use a little-c example, may spend his days immersed in studying and analyzing the various makes and models, engine styles, and performance options, sketching new car designs and imagining new features—to the exclusion of all other topics or areas of potential interest. Is this a problem? Sometimes. It certainly can be if a creative person's energy and interest in his endeavor negatively impact other parts of his life, such as family or work obligations, relationships, and school or job performance. Yet this kind of diligent persistence is necessary for the creative process and product to unfold.

Parents need to understand the energy, dedication, and persistence that creativity often requires and allow their children to engage in them. However, if children become so engrossed in a project that it becomes disruptive to other important aspects of their life, adults may need to step in and set some limits.

High Energy

Persistence requires high energy. It is not surprising that *driving absorption*, *passionate interest*, *intense dedication*, and *an unwillingness to give up* are all phrases used to describe the energy, perseverance, commitment, and motivation of highly creative individuals. Their intense energy and drive are noticeable in early childhood and are maintained into adulthood. Most creative accomplishments are not the result of a single spontaneous event or an overnight discovery, but rather a lifetime of work and commitment to a particular field or endeavor. Anders Ericcson found that talent requires commitment—10 years or 10,000 hours to become an expert in a field (2006). The roots of this persistence can be seen in the energy (and time) that young, creative children devote to their projects, often forgetting about lunch and play dates with friends because they are so engrossed and absorbed.

A creative child's energy can be both overt and covert. Overt energy is hard to miss, as it comes with behavior and intensity that can be "in your face," hard to keep up with, and exhausting. Covert, or quiet, energy is seen in children who are able to read, create, investigate, or study their interest of the moment, month, or year quietly and for hours on end. Either way, their intense energy, along with their persistence, is a primary contributor to their creative exploration.

Independence

Independence is central to creativity. The creative individual must be ready and willing to go against the crowd and at times to stand alone. We often use the euphemism "She marches to the beat of her own drum" as a way to describe someone who is creative in viewpoint, appearance, activities, or a host of other personal choices; someone who chooses to stand apart from others in various ways. Sometimes independence emerges in children in the form of direct challenges to parents, teachers, or other authority figures. We often hear parents say that their creative child likes to refute others' comments. Parents and teachers need to be understanding and accepting in order to help facilitate the creative tendency of an independent, strong-willed child while also setting appropriate boundaries and limits.

As George Bernard Shaw states in *Maxims for Revolutionists*, "The reasonable man adapts himself to the world; the unreasonable one persists in trying to adapt the world to himself. Therefore, all progress depends on the unreasonable man." It is the independence of thought that we often find difficult to deal with in creative individuals, and yet it is also what we celebrate when their creativity is responsible for an acceptable, useful outcome. We must remember that the "unreasonable" man or woman was first a boy or girl who was likely expressing his or her creativity and independence at a very young age.

> *Mateo is known as "The Contrarian" in his family. If someone says that something is black, he will argue that it is white. He refuses to do what is asked of him in the way that his parents and teacher ask him to do it. He puts a great deal of energy into proving his point and completing a task his way, which brings him an almost smug satisfaction. Always pushing the envelope, he turns everything into a debate, which is often seen as an argument about why his way is better and everyone else's way is insufficient.*

The ability to think independently is a positive trait; however, some creative children get into trouble if they push too far and fail to respect others' views. Parents and teachers do well to help these children learn to do a "cost-benefit analysis" when it comes to pushing their ideas. Children need to understand that sometimes forcing an idea on someone else or insisting on doing things a certain way comes with ramifications that simply are not worth the effort. In addition, parents and teachers should help independent-thinking children learn how to present facts to support their views and opinions—giving weight to their arguments and encouraging them to include others in their vision. The point is not to shut down the child's independence, but rather to help the child use it for worthwhile endeavors and, optimally, to do so in a way that turns others on to the new ideas rather than off to them.

Risk Taking

An individual who is independent is one who also is willing to take risks. Creativity brings with it at least a modicum of risk taking, including intellectual, social, psychological, emotional, and, yes, at times, even physical risks. (Think of the Wright brothers, César Chávez, Marie Curie, and Martin Luther King, Jr.) Whenever a person ventures a unique approach or opinion, that individual risks rejection, ridicule, or even isolation. Those who are highly physical or talented in the bodily-kinesthetic realm—for example, ballet dancers, gymnasts, or competitive divers—may be inclined to take physical risks in creative ways as well. It is essential that adults provide an environment that supports unique views and opportunities for risk taking while also reasonably assuring physical and psychological safety.

> *Kendra is a 16-year-old who has always been provocative in her self-expression. More recently she has been fascinated with tattoos and body piercings. She wants her parents to sign a consent form for her to get a tattoo and allow her to have large gauges (holes) put in her earlobes, as well as piercings in her eyebrows and nose. Her parents are trying to find a way to allow her self-expression while not permitting her to do anything permanent to her body that she may later regret. They are hoping to compromise by letting her dye and cut her hair and allowing an extra ear pierce. They know she will be free to make her own decisions in a few years.*

What can parents do in this kind of situation? We often tell parents that it can be helpful to explain the consequences of risks like these by having the child think through possible reactions from others. What will be the social costs of purple hair, if any? Teachers and students may think she is weird. Others may make assumptions about her that are undesirable, such as that she embraces taboo activities that she may in fact reject. Employers might not hire her when she applies for a job. What are the benefits? She will be expressing her independence and courage to go against the grain by modifying her appearance in a way that pleases her. Will there be any long-term costs or benefits? She can dye her hair back to a normal color easily enough, whereas a large hole in her ear might be permanent, and a tattoo almost certainly is.

At times, limits *are* necessary. If you set a limit for your child, it is not likely to take away or stifle her creativity forever, although it may create a disruption (hopefully short-lived) in your relationship for a time. We discuss limits in more depth later in this book.

Curiosity

Open-mindedness naturally leads to curiosity and questioning, and the creative impulse inclines one toward exploration and investigation. "How does this work?" "How can we make it better?" "Why is it like that?" "Can it be like this instead?" "Why couldn't we do it this way also?" This kind of question compels curious and creative children to seek understand of, interact with, and change within aspects of their environment.

Curiosity is a wonderful trait that we certainly want to nurture and develop. Yet when a teacher is trying to finish a lesson and has only 10 minutes, or a parent is trying to cook dinner, finish the laundry, and pack lunches for the next day, a long string of questions from a child can seem overwhelming. One strategy that parents and teachers often find successful for stemming the barrage of questions or keeping a lesson on track is the technique of having the child keep an "I/Q" sheet or journal. The "I" represents Important Ideas, and the "Q" stands for Questions. The child can record important thoughts and questions to save for a later discussion. This is a way of valuing a child's curiosity while also providing a management strategy that can be utilized to save the flood of questions or ideas for a time when the adult can give the child his or her full attention.

Sense of Humor/Playfulness

Humor is associated with an ability to approach problems—and life in general—in a fresh, childlike, and playful manner. Humor in the form of puns, satire, and farce engages the imagination by approaching topics with an unusual twist. A unique juxtaposition of ideas, words, and images often lends a humorous note to creative products. Numerous inventions and creations have resulted from fooling around with ideas and playing with possibilities, in contrast to more rule-bound approaches and traditions.

Whenever we give talks about creativity in children, we ask the hypothetical question, "Can you imagine having Whoopie Goldberg, Jim Carey, Tina Fey, and Robin Williams all in the same classroom or at the dinner table together?" These individuals express their divergence through their awareness of absurdities and contradictions in the world. They are creative in their use of puns, ironies, and commentary on people and situations. It is their willingness to be playful in their approach to their lives and work that contributes to the expression of their creativity.

Undoubtedly, Pete Davidson, Amy Schumer, and other popular humorists took on the role of class clown when they were in school. However, teachers don't usually appreciate class clowns because they disrupt the class and detract from the lesson. Like curiosity, humor is a trait that can be double-edged. So how can parents and teachers accept and appreciate the clown or jokester in the room, admire his talent, his wit, and his skill and yet still maintain some sense of order? It helps if parents and teachers can laugh, too, and then defuse the situation and come back to the task at hand. To constantly send the disruptive jokester to the principal's office is not likely to help matters much; it may only serve to give him more attention and power. It may be best to just let the joke play out and then get on with things. If a teacher or parent can appreciate a good joke, then the jokester is more likely to give the adult "her turn" when the joke is over. Of course, jokes should never be hurtful or at the expense of others.

We are reminded of a story about Mike Peters, editorial cartoonist for many years for the *Dayton Daily News*. Mr. Peters won a Pulitzer Prize in 1981 for his editorial cartoons. However, when he was in high school, his assistant principal wrote in his yearbook, "You'd better grow up, Mr. Peters! You can't always draw cartoons." To this day, Mr. Peters makes a good living from his syndicated cartoon *Mother Goose and Grimm*, which exemplifies his zany sense of humor. Indeed, it appears that he *can* always draw cartoons!

Attraction to Complexity

Creativity is not a simple concept or process. Often creative enterprises bridge disciplines, styles, materials, techniques, cultures, geography, and time periods. Creative people tend to be drawn to complexity, and creative children often enjoy making the simple complex. Thus, an environment that is rich and varied in resources, materials, and modes of interaction will support and may contribute to an increase in creative activity.

Christian and his Collection of Contraptions from Chapter 1 is a perfect example of a child deliberately making things more complex. Christian's contraptions are reminiscent of the Rube Goldberg conundrums, in which complex machines perform simple tasks. It is interesting to note that Rube Goldberg (yes, he was an actual person) was trained as an engineer at the University of California at Berkeley in the early 1900s and then began working for a newspaper drawing cartoons—clearly a creative twist in his career.

In his book *Creativity: Flow and the Psychology of Discovery and Invention*, Mihaly Csikszentmihalyi (1997) studied many accomplished and world-changing scientists, writers, and artists (1997). Most of those individuals described drawing from several disciplines when investigating, creating, and ultimately producing their new invention, formula, book, or product. During the creative process, they were driven to dive deeply into their own field, but also into related fields as well.

It is important to remember that for creative individuals, complexity, like the other traits described in this chapter, is not a choice. It is often the result of their divergent and elaborate thinking as they strive for understanding and make connections. Whether you are raising another Christian, with his odd collection of mechanical items, or an Albert Einstein, complexity for creative individuals appears to be the rule rather than the exception.

Even if at times it seems bewildering or frustrating, parents and teachers should accept and embrace the complexity in creative children. It would be sad if Christian's mother refused to let him keep his assortment of broken appliances. The fact that she allows him to collect those things is her way of supporting his passion and interest.

Artistic Interests and Aesthetic Perspectives

The creativity studies of Mihaly Csikszentmihalyi indicate that people who are engaged in a creative career and creative pursuits have personality and values differences when compared to others. The more original the art student, the more extreme are her standards of a personal aesthetic. Similarly, many creative scientists value a sense of aesthetics and elegance over commercial reward or recognition.

This personal sense of aesthetics is apparent in even very young creative children. For instance, a five-year-old girl insists upon mismatching her socks, shoes, and gloves, anything that comes in a pair. Or a four-year-old boy who chooses to don a dress shirt and bow tie for preschool but will only wear flipflops on his feet because he doesn't like to have his toes covered. A second-grade girl brings a handmade card to her teacher every morning. A kindergarten student keeps an invention design log.

It is important to note that while these children may have an artistic bent and a heightened sense of aesthetics, this does not necessarily mean that they have artistic talent. It does mean that they may notice form, color, sound, and aesthetic aspects of their world to a greater extent than others.

Sensitivity and Intensity

Kazimierz Dabrowski, a Polish psychologist and psychiatrist, worked with and studied the development of gifted, talented, and creative youth. He discovered that these young people were far more sensitive and intense than their less gifted, talented, and creative peers. Dabrowski found that this sensitivity and intensity, this capacity to be intensely stimulated and to stay stimulated—which he termed *overexcitability*—provides fuel for creative development (Daniels & Piechowski, 2009).

Overexcitability is an innate tendency to respond in an intensified manner to various forms of stimuli, both external and internal. The word is translated from a Polish term that literally means "super-stimulatability." This means that less stimulation is required both to produce a response and to sustain the intensity of the response. Dabrowski identified five forms of overexcitability that contribute to the development of creativity and giftedness:

- *Psychomotor*—movement; restlessness; drivenness; an augmented capacity for being active and energetic
- *Sensual*—enhanced refinement and aliveness of sensual experience, including sights, sounds, smells, tastes, and textures

- *Intellectual*—thirst for knowledge, discovery, questioning; love of ideas and theoretical analysis; search for understanding
- *Imaginational*—vividness of imagery; richness of association; facility for dreams, fantasies, and inventions; endowing toys and other objects with personality; preference for the unusual and unique
- *Emotional*—great depth and intensity of emotions expressed in a wide range of feelings, from elation to profound sadness or despair, to compassion and self-reflection

One can see how a child with one or more of these overexcitabilities can be enjoyable, interesting, alive, almost vibrating with excitement, but also can be complex, challenging, at times annoying, and difficult or troublesome. Parents and teachers who understand that a child's gifts and talents come with the complexities of overexcitability will better be able to accept and nurture that child.

Overexcitabilities can be sources of great pleasure and joy but also can overwhelm and cause discomfort. Jane Piirto, author of *Understanding Creativity*, talks about the creative thorn, explaining that sometimes we need to feel a bit of a prick from without or within to feel moved to create (2004). This notion fits with the concept of overexcitability. The book *Living with Intensity* develops this idea further and includes a wealth of information for parents to help their children build on the positive potential inherent in an overexcitable nature while also managing and modulating its challenges (Daniels & Piechowski, 2009).

Perception

There Was a Child Went Forth Every Day

There was a child went forth every day;

And the first object he look'd upon, that object he became;

And that object became part of him for the day, or a certain part of the day, or for many years, or stretching cycles of years.

The early lilacs became part of this child,

And grass, and white and red morning-glories, and white and red clover, and the song of the phoebe-bird,

And the third month lambs, and the sow's pink-faint litter, and the mare's foal, and the cow's calf,

And the noisy brood of the barn-yard, or by the mire of the pond-side,

And the fish suspending themselves so curiously below there—and the beautiful curious liquid,

And the water-plants with their graceful flat heads—all became part of him.

~ Walt Whitman

Whitman's poem beautifully captures much of what we know about creativity in children. For children, life itself is a creative adventure. Their overexcitabilities heighten their responses to the world around them. Every sight, smell, taste, sound, and touch has creative potential. Exploring the world through one's senses and perceptions is essential creative work for young children. What is significant is that creative children and adults notice and are more aware of their perceptions. They contemplate these perceptions and, as we will discuss later, often mentally play with them.

Unfortunately, many children today do not have access to nature or the natural world, which contains an enormous source of perceptual stimulation that engages all the senses. Books have been written on what has come to be called *nature-deficit disorder* (Louv, 2005). This is an informal diagnosis, yet it is highly descriptive of the experiences of many children. All too often, children who live in large urban centers or sprawling suburbs do not have access to the lush, verdant landscapes and mindscapes of the natural world. Even children in rural areas who have too much screen time—i.e., time spent in front of televisions, computers, and gaming devices—may miss out on the experiences that the out-of-doors can present.

Adults can help overcome the disconnect between children and the natural world with fieldtrips and vacations, which have the potential for powerful and lasting impact. One of this book's authors, Susan, taught at an inner-city school that was just two miles from a beach. Startlingly, the majority of the children in the school were neither aware that the beach was there, nor had they ever visited it. A fieldtrip was arranged, and the children engaged in sampling, drawing, writing about, discussing, and discovering the natural environment of the beach.

Sometimes, if we get too caught up in our busy schedules, we forget how invigorating—in terms our senses, our thinking, our emotions, and our creative responsiveness—such day trips can be. Most of us have not been to all of the nature centers, preserves, state and national parks, or wildlife sanctuaries near us. We can encourage our children's independence and planning skills by allowing them to choose one of these places to visit and help plan the outing. Once there, we can watch as our children's perceptions evolve and sharpen.

Awareness of Creativity

Perception isn't just about noticing one's surroundings. Creative individuals tend to be aware of their own creativity as well, and this awareness can lead to a heightened awareness of the creativity of others. This self-awareness is called *metacognition*—i.e., thinking about one's thinking—and such a metacognitive understanding of creativity is usually self-reinforcing. That is, a "creativity consciousness" is receptive to and values creative ideas and innovations, and it seems to underlie and support an individual's creative potential.

Creative individuals are attracted to novelty. They notice and appreciate things, ideas, and people who are different and purposeful. Whereas less innately creative individuals may prefer to do the same things in the same ways and even at the same times, creative individuals seek out what is unusual, extraordinary, whimsical, unique, and different in the environment. This can include a wide range of materials, artifacts, and experiences, including toys, statues, clothing, graphic design, theater, and more. And these creative folks also seek ways to inject more creativity wherever an opportunity allows. For example, creative children may take a prefab model of a car or a plane or a fort or a house and create their own version of it, varying the design greatly rather than following the directions. This is an aspect of individualizing and increasing novelty as a part of the creative process.

Creative individuals are constantly thinking about possibilities and noticing creativity in their surroundings. Their inclination toward this type of thinking allows more opportunities for creative ideas to incubate, develop, and reach expression.

Boosting Creative Potential—For Ourselves and Our Children

While all creative individuals are different, they tend to possess many, if not all, of the characteristics discussed in this chapter. These traits are innate, but they also can be nurtured and developed. It is these characteristics that impact children's thoughts, ideas, behaviors, and experiences, often resulting in unique expressions of art or innovative approaches and solutions to problems in the world around them.

How many of the characteristics does your child have? How many of them contribute to her uniqueness, and also to her challenging behavior? How can you nurture these creative characteristics in your child—and in yourself?

As an adult, being aware of and striving to nurture your own creativity will help you to support your child's creative development. Engaging in even small, everyday creative acts yourself will provide a great starting point to connect to and to help you boost your child's creativity. For example, you can:

- **Be childlike.** In our busy lives, it can be a challenge to take time and notice the beauty of our surroundings. We encourage you to grab hold of the everyday opportunities to take delight in our world and in our surroundings. Try to take time—even five or ten minutes each day—to smell the flowers, literally; take out a pen and a small notebook and doodle what you see or sit with your child and watch the sunset. What other creative moments can you find—or make—in your day?

- **Be open to new experiences.** Try something new that will help you to stay openminded and keep your thinking fresh. Take a different route to work or to the store. Pay attention to differences in your surroundings. Wear a hat or a piece of clothing you haven't worn before. Change up a recipe that you've made before by swapping some of the ingredients.
- **Foster a playful attitude.** Enjoy the intrinsic pleasure of playing with your children. Follow their lead, tell different stories, use different materials. Dance together in the living room. Use your vegetables as spontaneous puppets before combining them in your salad!!
- **Read about creative people, their work and the things that inspired them.** Many artists, scientists and inventors have stories about powerful opportunities they had for learning and playing, special places where they would go to imagine and create, and how the adults in their lives would provide them the freedom to explore their surroundings in new and different ways

Keep reading! You'll find more ideas and suggestions for playing and growing creatively in the chapters to come.

Chapter 4
The Creative Teen *Or* "Excuse Me, Have You Seen My Child?"

You thought your young creative child was intense and complex. Just wait for adolescence! What a challenging time for both parent and teen! So many changes are happening in your adolescent's brain and body that unpredictability and emotionality seem like the norm during this period of life. Hormones are surging, creating physical changes and intense emotions that seem to demand unbridled expression. In addition, adolescence is a time of prolific brain development, which also affects your child's emotions and behaviors. It's a time of great changes and potentially a time for considerable personal creativity!

Brain Development and Adolescence

Whereas we once thought that the brain reached full development during childhood, recent advances in brain science have taught us that the brain is not fully developed until age 20 to 25. In her book *Brain Matters: Translating Research into Classroom Practice*, international brain educator Pat Wolfe (2010) describes how the brain goes through a second bout of the "terrible twos" during adolescence. Researchers have known for some time that the brain experiences prolific cell grown when a child is very young. Dr. Wolfe extends these findings describing a study by the National Institute of Mental Health (NIMH) that found that just prior to puberty (ages 9-10), the frontal lobes (the large part of the brain behind our forehead that is responsible for planning, judgment, and managing our emotions and behavior) undergo a second wave of reorganization and growth, representing millions of new neural connections. Next comes a period of *pruning* at around age 11, during which extra brain cells that are not used wither and die, while neural connections that are used more often stay strong, increasing brain efficiency.

In addition to increased cell growth and pruning, a process called *myelination* occurs. Myelin is the "laminated wrapping" that covers many of the nerve fibers of our brain cells, speeding up electrical impulses and allowing for efficient communication among neurons. You could think of myelination as a sort of insulation around specific connections. For instance, if we learn to play a song on the piano, our neurons form connections between the different parts of the brain that affect how we read the sheet music, how we move our fingers, and how we hear the notes. When we practice that song, those connections get stronger, and ultimately myelination occurs. We sit down and play the song again and again, and soon we realize that we don't need to look at the sheet music anymore. Maybe we don't even need to look at our fingers. We just close our eyes and let our fingers do what they have become so adept at doing—playing a song that we have memorized so well because our brain has created a strong set of connecting cells that enable us to do so.

Dr. Wolfe described another study that compared the brains of young adults (ages 20-23) to those of teens (ages 12-16), looking for signs of myelin that would suggest more mature and efficient connections as one ages. Not surprisingly, the teenage brain showed less myelination than the young adult brain. It is now thought that full myelination does not occur until possibly age 30 or even later! All of this information helps us to understand that the adolescent brain is a "work in progress." It might help if you imagine your adolescent walking around with scaffolding around his brain, with little construction workers milling around and signs all over the scaffolding saying "Caution: Under Construction. Enter at your own risk!"

Within the brain, the frontal lobes and the area right behind the frontal lobes, collectively called the prefrontal cortex, are the last to fully develop. These parts are often thought of as the "CEO" of the brain. The CEO functions of the prefrontal cortex include:

- Organizing multiple tasks
- Setting goals and priorities
- Inhibiting specific impulses
- Maintaining self-control
- Empathizing with others
- Initiating appropriate behavior
- Making sound judgments
- Forming strategies
- Planning ahead
- Adjusting behavior based on changing situations
- Stopping an activity based on completion

Now remember, these skills and abilities are regulated by the last part of the brain to mature, which means that your teenager may be smart and sensitive, funny and creative, but she likely will be lacking in the areas of judgment, analysis, evaluation, and prioritizing. This list probably helps to answer a question you may have asked in response to your teen's behavior on more than one occasion: "What were you thinking?" The answer is that she *wasn't* thinking, just doing. The parts of her brain that control her emotions have matured much faster than the parts that direct rational, logical thought. Her brain literally isn't developed enough for her to be thinking in certain ways yet.

The prefrontal cortex seems to be responsible for all of the behaviors that adolescents are known to lack. We will be talking more about the CEO functions of the brain and how to help your child develop these thinking abilities later in the book, so please know that while your child may have weaknesses in these areas, there are many things you can do to help her improve.

Isn't it interesting that adolescence—a time when your child so badly wants increased independence—is a time of growth and changes in the brain that actually limit her ability to be independent? You may be wondering when all this cell growth, pruning, and myelination is going to occur in your teen and whether you can speed it up. Sorry, there is no rushing development. Kids' brains mature on their own schedule. The good news is that it *will* happen at some point. The bad news is that until then, parents must learn to breathe deeply and hang on for the ride!

Devon

> *Devon is 14 and an eighth grader. He has developed a passion and skill for metalwork and blacksmithing. In fact, that is what he prefers to do with most of his free time. He is known in his community for his skill and is sought after to make personalized pieces—knives, wind chimes, and hardware for cabinetry. Devon is well-liked by the adults he meets. He can carry on conversations about virtually any topic and is mature in his thinking and his ability to articulate his thoughts. He can literally speak with someone for hours.*
>
> *Devon's experiences with school have been mixed. He often is teased and bullied by the other middle schoolers. He longs for peer connection but has a difficult time finding others his age with whom he can relate. He finds many of his peers to be immature in their interests and behaviors. Ironically, while he is mature and adult-like in many ways, Devon seems immature and childlike to his peers. He tends to be very direct, saying whatever comes to his mind. He doesn't think there is a problem in expressing his thoughts, even if it offends others.*

Devon has a difficult time concentrating on and doing his schoolwork. Instead, he finds himself thinking about his next metalwork project or his engineering ideas that involve producing natural, sustainable power.

Devon's relationship with his parents is mixed as well. He vacillates between wanting complete independence and seeming dependent on them to help him complete his homework and regular daily tasks like getting up in the morning for school and going to bed at a reasonable hour. Devon has unpredictable, strong emotional reactions when he is not allowed to do what he wants and when he is unable to complete a task that he knows he should do, such as finishing his homework. His parents are perplexed by his vacillation between rational, high-level thinking and childlike temper tantrums.

Sabrina

Sabrina is 13 and in seventh grade. She has always had her own style. Some refer to her as "Pippi Longstocking" because of her colorful and seemingly random choices of outfits. Sabrina, however, is very purposeful in her selection of clothing, choosing particular patterns and mixing and matching genres. She knows she has her own style and is proud of it. She simply can't imagine dressing like everyone or anyone else. Most of her peers are not sure what to make of her. They seem to respect that she is an individual but find her hard to relate to, and she often seems immature to them.

Sabrina has a talent for art. She has been drawing, painting, and sculpting for several years. Her room is her studio, with magazine clippings, household items, and various art supplies spread across her worktable and floor. She works in her room for hours on end, often well into the night. There is a narrow path between all of her "art supplies" that allows her to get to her bed, dresser, and bathroom. She works with a mentor once a week to learn more about art mediums, as well as the business of selling art and dealing with customers.

> *While confident in her creative pursuits, Sabrina is shy, anxious, and lacks confidence in navigating the world. Because of some significant learning disabilities, she has struggled tremendously in school and has always felt dumb. This, along with her shy personality, has left her feeling anxious around others, and she gets very emotional when she feels she is unable to manage her schoolwork or her social relationships. Although she frequently demonstrates a mature perspective on life when she is not hampered by her anxieties, Sabrina sometimes exhibits an immaturity that surprises her parents, such as using expensive or meaningful household items for her art without asking first. Her parents are not sure which Sabrina will "show up" at any given moment—the anxious child or the mature young adult.*

Dualities within the Creative Brain

Do Devon and Sabrina sound familiar? Are you thinking about them—or your own teenager—a little differently now that you have a better understanding of what is occurring in their brains? Both Devon and Sabrina, who are quite advanced and confident in their creative endeavors, nevertheless can be emotional and seem to have difficulty organizing certain aspects of their lives. They both act impulsively at times as well. Would it help if their parents knew that these behaviors were related to their developing brains? We think so.

Although dealing with your adolescent's behavior may be difficult, having an understanding of why he acts in the ways he does can help calm some parental worries and can build a bit more patience, tolerance, and empathy.

While knowing about brain development is critical for understanding your adolescent's behavior, so too is understanding his personality characteristics. In previous chapters, you learned about the characteristics of creative people, and you likely recognized several of those traits in your child. We'd now like to share more personality characteristics with you that may help to better explain your creative teen. In his book *Creativity: Flow and the Psychology of Discovery and Invention*, Mihaly Csikszentmihalyi (1997) described the "psychic complexity" of creative individuals, stating that they have the ability "to move from one trait to its opposite." Lisa Rivero (2010), in her book *A Parent's Guide to Gifted Teens: Living with Intense and Creative Adolescents*, nicely summarizes these 10 dualities as follows:

1. *Energetic and restful*: Creative people can have both sustained bursts of energy and deep periods of rest.
2. *Intelligent and naïve*: Creative people are both extremely smart about some things and surprisingly innocent and naive about others.
3. *Playful and disciplined*: Creative people have both a zany (divergent) and straightforward (convergent) side.
4. *Fanciful and reality-based*: Creative people have one foot in the clouds and the other on the ground.
5. *Humble and proud*: Creative people are not driven by their egos and may even shy from publicity or recognition, but they also accept and are glad for their gifts and accomplishments.
6. *Masculine and feminine*: Creative people tend to be androgynous. They exhibit both traditional male and female traits, such as assertiveness and tenderness (note that this dimension has nothing to do with sexual identity or preference).
7. *Rebellious and conservative*: Creative people are not afraid to break with the status quo, yet at other times they stick with tradition.
8. *Passionate and objective*: Creative people can fall in love with the world while still seeing the world as it is.
9. *Suffering and blissful*: Creative people know and feel suffering without losing a sense of joy and wonder.
10. *Introverted and extroverted*: Creative people are comfortable being by themselves but also can learn and use skills of interdependence.

These dualities were found to be inherent in eminently creative individuals who have had a significant impact on our world through their contributions in the areas of science, medicine, psychology, leadership, business, literature, and art. Although the characteristics were derived from adults, they also apply to adolescents who are in the process of becoming adults. We feel that it is helpful to understand the "usual" characteristics of creative individuals so that they can be recognized and accepted as normal for a creative teen rather than judged for being worrisome or showing some kind of pathology.

Admittedly, these dualities were seen in accomplished creative individuals who were able to take their ideas (divergence) and produce something (convergence) that had a significant impact on our world. But while all of the individuals that Csikszentmihalyi studied ultimately ended up producing at the Big-C level, we can be sure that they were engaging in many mini-c and little-c behaviors long before they went on to Pro-c ones.

Let's take a closer look at some of the dual characteristics of creative individuals through the examples of Devon and Sabrina. First, consider the idea of being both energetic and restful. Both Devon and Sabrina are known to work on their forms of art for extended periods of time with intense focus and seemingly tireless energy. When this occurs, they often lose track of time, forgetting their regular day-to-day obligations such as homework, karate, tutoring, chores, and family meals. On the other hand, both Devon and Sabrina are known to retreat to quiet places in their homes for down time and "mindless" activities like playing video games and watching television. Sabrina likes to get lost in a fantasy novel, while Devon likes to read about inventors and explorers. That down time can last for an afternoon, but it also may extend to a week or even a month, during which both teens go without engaging in their creative pursuit. Their parents find themselves vacillating between telling them that they are obsessing over their projects at the expense of the rest of their obligations and worrying that they are becoming lazy and are no longer passionate about their areas of interest.

Next let's take a look at the dichotomy of being both intelligent and naïve. As their vignettes point out, both Devon and Sabrina often come across as older than they actually are in terms of the ways in which they communicate with adults and the advanced topics they think about. At the same time, they are seen by their classmates as immature and innocent because they don't fit in with their age peers and are not focused on more "adult" social pursuits like dating. This duality can be confusing to individuals like Devon and Sabrina because they feel mature on many levels, yet they don't seem to have interests similar to those of their peers, and they may secretly wonder if there is something wrong with them. Intellectually, Devon and Sabrina see their peers as immature, but their peers are judging them socially and are thinking quite the opposite. Their parents are often perplexed that these two teens seem mature and immature at the same time.

Devon and Sabrina also have aspects of being both humble and proud. Each feels confident in his or her abilities, with no need to boast about them. When they do discuss their metalwork and art, they do so through their passion and interest, hoping to find others who may understand and appreciate their work as they do. This is why creative adolescents often relate well to older teens and adults who share and can appreciate their forms of creative expression.

The notion of exhibiting both male and female traits is important as well. Creative youth tend to be more in touch with and more able to express both masculine and feminine characteristics. This is not about sexual preference. Instead, it is the ability for a male, for instance, to be in tune with and be able to accurately convey his emotions, as well as to have an understanding of and appreciation for aesthetics typically attributed to females. As well, it may mean that a female might express more stereotypical male characteristics of assertiveness and risk taking. During adolescence, which includes both hormonal development and identity development, it is important to allow creative teens to be comfortable with who they are and to not unintentionally give them messages about what is "male" and "female" behavior or how they are "supposed" to be or act. Gender stereotypic messages abound at school and from the media, so parents and others should try to counteract these messages with acceptance and an open mind.

The issue of being both rebellious and conservative also applies to Devon and Sabrina. Both of them push the limits of convention in their art and personal expression. Devon experiments with ways to produce heat on his forge that are sometimes dangerous and directly against his parents' rules about safety. Sabrina, as well, has damaged family property while trying to put together an artistic creation, and she pushes the convention of dress. On the other hand, both Devon and Sabrina are known to have high moral and ethical values that are seen as conservative to their peers. They are clear about what is right and wrong, and they rarely cross that line unless they have a momentary lapse of judgment.

The idea of knowing suffering while also being blissful is an interesting duality seen in creative individuals. Imagine the suffering artist who feels deep pain and sadness while also seeing the beauty in nature and art. We have found this to be true for many of the creative teens we have worked with. One example is Finn, a 15-year-old who believes in self-expression at all costs. Finn finds wonder and passion in music, and he feels that music can provide the most powerful form of healing. In fact, he writes music with the goal of helping others find understanding, meaning, and relief. It is logical, then, to conclude that Finn cannot have this goal without empathizing with the depths of pain and sorrow that others sometimes experience. Indeed, Finn feels deeply and has suffered from his own feelings of sadness, isolation, and exclusion. Anyone who spends time with him can see how he vacillates between his awe of music, as well as the hope it brings, and the sadness he feels from his own experiences.

Finally, the duality of introversion and extraversion is worth describing further, particularly for how it often relates to adolescent development. Some children seem always to have been introverted, while others are extraverted as children but somehow turn into introverted teens. The differentiating factor with introversion and extraversion is where a person derives his energy. The introvert generally feels recharged after spending time alone or with one or two close friends or family members, whereas the extravert generally gets an energy boost from being with others. It is not uncommon for an adolescent to become more private and need more personal space during this developmental period. Remember, this is a very confusing time, with significant brain and body changes occurring simultaneously.

It is important to understand your teen's predominant personality style—introversion or extraversion. Knowing whether he craves contact or needs some alone time can help you better understand his personal needs and navigate potential conflict points related to his activity schedule, his social life, and his family commitments. The duality of introversion and extraversion in creative individuals also suggests that your teen may express his less dominant style at times as well. For example, Devon is seen as very social with adults and loves to talk for hours with individuals who share his metalwork interest. On the other hand, he is shy around his peers and often describes feeling depleted after attending school or a social activity.

An important finding in Csikszentmihalyi's study of creative people was that many of the introverted individuals were able to learn how to be more extraverted and how better to relate to others. In fact, how they related to others often directly correlated with their creative product, as they needed to collaborate with others along the way to discovery. So, there is good news: Your extremely extraverted and high-energy teen can have moments of calm and reflection, and your very shy and introverted teen can be interactive and connect well with others.

Asynchrony

We want to discuss a final concept that is closely related to the development of the creative adolescent. This concept is called *asynchrony*, otherwise known as uneven development. Because different parts of the brain develop at different times, children and teenagers can show a wide range of emotional, intellectual, and physical levels of development. The more creative the child, the wider the diversity tends to be.

Developmental asynchrony is useful for understanding the complexities of your creative teen's often quirky and seemingly unpredictable behavior. Imagine yourself as the parent of a 12-yearold who has the artistic or musical ability of an 18-year-old, the vocabulary skills of a 16-year-old, the emotional control of an eight-year-old, and the organization skills of a six-year-old. This complex human being, your much-loved child, encompasses several developmental levels all at once. Which one will show up at any given time? That's a good question. The answer is that you probably can anticipate which one will show up depending on the situation at hand. "How many times do I have to tell you to clean up your last project before starting a new one?" That would be the six-year old. "How can you expect us to treat you like an teenager if you scream and cry when you don't get what you want?" That sounds like the eight-year-old. "Look, you can make the best arguments in the world, but I'm not buying that plasma TV for your room!" That's the eloquence of the 16-year-old. "Wow, they said they want you to join the junior symphony, even though they'll have to bend the rules because you're technically too young? That's incredible!" That would be your 18-year-old. And all of those kids are housed in one body! The point is that your creative teen has several areas of functioning that are developing at different levels all at once. And she is likely to be just as perplexed about it as you are.

Here's a helpful hint for distressed parents of asynchronous teens: Even though your teen is functioning at different levels simultaneously, it is never helpful to point out when a "younger version" is present. ("You are acting like an eight-year-old!") On the other hand, it could be helpful to have a conversation with your teen about her development at a time when it seems appropriate—for example, when she's calm and amenable, but not when she's feeling overly emotional or when you are in the midst of a power struggle. More parenting strategies to help you deal with your intense youngster appear in the next chapter.

Boosting Creative Potential During the Teenage Years

You started with a child who thought differently and uniquely and seemed to have his own ideas about the way things should be. Now you are parenting an adolescent who still has his own way of doing things but demands even more independence while possibly pushing the limits of convention even further. To make matters even more challenging, your teen doesn't seem able to regularly fulfill his home and school obligations. What's more, he's highly emotional and often irrational. Welcome to parenting a creative teen.

"So now what?" you may be asking yourself. We have several strategies that we share in our parenting chapter, which comes later in the book. For now, however, the important thing to remember is that your creative teen has a *lot* going on in his brain, as well as in his body, and he is often as confused by his emotions and behaviors as you are. Further, it is important to remember that although your teen may seem like he is never going to "grow up, take responsibility for his behavior, and think about someone else other than himself," he *will* grow up. Adolescence is a developmental phase that is time-limited, even though it can last more than a decade! Sigh. Try to remember that an adolescent is a work in progress, but then again, aren't we all?

Chapter 5
Creative Activities for Boosting Creative Thinking

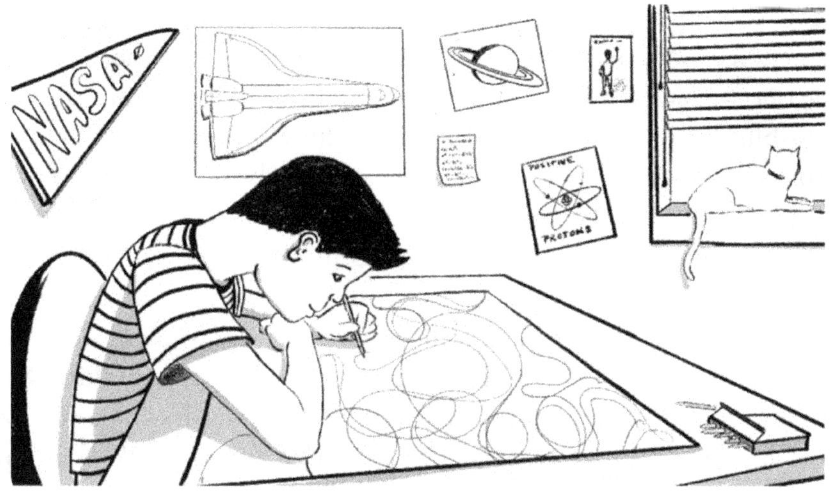

Creative people often see things differently from the way others see them. They think differently, they observe more keenly, and they notice things that others miss.

One key aspect of creativity is divergent thinking—a way of thinking that generates many different thoughts, ideas, or potential solutions to problems. Divergent thinkers enjoy and even prefer the unusual, the unique, the original, and the creative aspects of life. They have a preference for novelty and variety. They embellish, rearrange, and change things up rather than sticking to a script or an agenda. They consider the possibilities.

Convergent thinkers, on the other hand, prefer regularity and the known over the unknown. Convergent thinkers do well in our current test-driven, "one right answer" school environments. They like to be organized and can be quite uncomfortable with uncertainty.

While most individuals have a preference for one style or the other—convergent or divergent thinking—the two are not mutually exclusive. People often use both kinds of thinking. In fact, bringing creativity to fruition in terms of an outcome or a product requires aspects of both divergent and convergent thinking.

It works like this: We engage in divergent thinking to discover unique perspectives and generate possible ideas. We then need to apply the skills of convergent thinking to make a selection among the choices we have envisioned, analyze them, and further develop the one we have chosen. We need divergent thinking to imagine the possibilities, and convergent thinking to move forward with an idea, project, or solution to a problem. It is the interplay of these two modes of thought that work together to bring creativity and innovation to fruition. For example, let's say that an individual wants to plant a vegetable garden to supply some of his fresh produce, but since he lives in an apartment, he has conceived of the idea to plant all of his vegetables in containers on his balcony. His divergent thinking has led him to a creative solution to his problem of not having a plot of land in which to plant, but he needs to use convergent thinking in order to make that plan a reality. He'll need to do some research to learn which vegetables grow easily in his geographic area, what type of soil they'll need, how much sun they'll need, and so on before he can have a successful "garden."

Table 5.1 summarizes the differing characteristics of convergent and divergent thinkers. Does your child have characteristics on each side of the list? Is one side a little heavier than the other? And how about you—where do the majority of your characteristics reside? Are you more of a convergent or a divergent thinker?

Table 5.1. Convergent Thinkers vs. Divergent Thinkers

Convergent Thinkers	Divergent Thinkers
Like to find the one right answer	Imagine many possible answers
Prefer to analyze concepts and take them apart	Synthesize ideas; put ideas together in new and novel combinations
Are good at following directions	Are open to creating multiple ideas and possibilities
Are orderly; prefer to finish one task before beginning another	Can work on several tasks simultaneously
Are particular, specific, and concrete	Think more abstractly and consider multiple perspectives and viewpoints
Prefer to organize tasks in a project in a sequential order	Have a global perspective; prefer to consider the whole project before deciding where to begin

Unfortunately for our children—and their creative potential—schools these days emphasize convergent thinking to the relative exclusion of divergent thinking, and at times, it seems the teacher, the curriculum, and the school culture itself actively work to suppress divergent thinking. In this chapter, we hope to offset the extra emphasis schools give to convergent thinking by describing a wide variety of divergent thinking skills and creative processes that parents can support and foster outside of school. These ideas also work well for teachers who want to give their students a more creative classroom experience.

So, get ready for a lot of information, ideas, and sample activities in the pages ahead. We are not suggesting that you follow our suggestions word for word or that you do every one of the activities; you'll need to select and adapt them as it suits you and your child. As a caring, conscientious, and creative parent, you already may be well on your way with many of these approaches and suggestions. If that's the case, think of this chapter as a source for ideas, and see what new thoughts they may spark in you. Some of the activities can be approached as games, for times when you have five extra minutes waiting in line or while driving in the car. Others require some preparation. But all of them are meant to be enjoyable and in no way are supposed to be presented as serious "homework." Have fun with them, and come back to this chapter when you want to try something new. We'll start with imagination. Here we go.

Imagination

A vivid imagination is one of the hallmark characteristics of a creative individual. Imaginative behavior is "what if" behavior. Children with vivid imaginations disregard the limitations of *what is* and instead think of *what might be*. They consider worlds of possibility in their everyday musings and day dreams. They make up imaginary characters that have imaginary conversations in imaginary worlds. Imagination is considered by some to be a whimsical pastime only for young children, but imagination is at the core of all artistic and scientific innovation.

While imagination has not held a place of high regard in our school curricula for the last several decades, Lev Vygotsky—an early and eminent developmental psychologist—considered it essential for all learning and development. He described two kinds of cognitive behaviors: those that are reproductive of our past experiences, which lack a creative quality, and those that he called imaginative. Imaginative behavior is based on the brain's ability to draw from, combine, and recombine elements from our previous experiences.

Vygotsky explored the power of the brain and described brain is not only the organ that stores and retrieves our previous experience; it is also the organ that combines and creatively reworks elements of this past experience and uses them to generate new propositions and new behavior.... This creative activity, based on the ability of our brain to combine elements, is called imagination or fantasy in psychology.

Some contemporary developmental and cognitive psychologists consider imagination to be central to all thought. How might we think about anything, really, without imagining a mental image or representation of the thing we wish to contemplate?

Parents can support—and boost—children's active imaginations by posing questions and engaging in imaginative play. They might ask, for example:

- What if dogs fit in the palm of your hand?
- What if people didn't walk but instead bounced like pogo sticks?
- What if people could fly like birds?
- What if insects could talk? What would they say to us?
    - What would a furry lollapalooza look like, and would it make a good pet?
    - If you were to have magic powers, what would they be? And what would you do?
- What if people were only two inches tall? What would the world look like to them? How would they live differently?

These and other questions will get children's imaginations engaged. You can even have them think up their own questions for double the imaginative play.

For a slightly different perspective, Charlotte Reznick (2009), in her book *The Power of Your Child's Imagination*, speaks of children using imagination, daydreaming, and fantasy as a way to create inner calm and peacefulness. Reznick emphasizes the inner worlds that children create—imaginary friends, imaginary places, and imaginary communities. These are reveries where children can create their own ideal experiences, not bounded by the concrete realities of the day-to-day. Many children naturally slip into this form of imagination, and some parents find that leading their children into an imagination activity with such statements as "Let's go to our special place" or "Let's take an imaginary trip together" are lovely ways to share imagination together at bedtime or when the child needs some quiet time.

Here is an example of how imagination and visualization might be used to soothe a child at bedtime.

> *Imagine yourself walking on a beautiful path lined with trees and flowers. It slopes gently downward and winds slightly to the left and the right. In the distance, you can hear the sound of waves, and after a moment or two, the path opens up to a clearing with your favorite cabin in the center. You open the*

> *carved wooden door and step through it. This is your special place. You can choose to take a nap here, you might read quietly to yourself and listen to soft music, or you might invite favorite friends and animals to join you. This is your special place. You can do anything you like or nothing at all. When you are ready, come back to your cozy bed and let yourself fall asleep naturally.*

Of course, parents can come up with their own prompts for different circumstances, or they can challenge their children to invent their own. This sort of imagination activity is satisfying and purposeful as a process to experience; it may not result in a project or product. Yet using the imagination within a restful context also potentially sets the scene for developing creative projects as they emerge from these imaginational ideations.

Awareness

We said earlier that creative people are good observers. They see things others may miss completely. Being aware, not just of our surroundings, but also of our own thoughts and feelings, gives us a steady supply of material for examination and reflection; the more we have to work with, the more prolific our ideas and solutions will be.

There are many different ways in which to be aware and observant, and in many different areas. One third-grade girl, Tiana, has a passion for color. She likes to collect flowers from her mother's garden—she loves flowers. She is highly aware of the nuanced shades of colors, and she saves the flowers as a sort of floral color palette, since she enjoys painting landscapes. Her sensory and imagery awareness is so sensitive and so acute that even when the colors lose their vibrancy after the flowers are dried and pressed, she claims that she can still recall their original shades and hues.

A first-grade boy, Marcus, likes to collect broken machines: hairdryers, toasters, vacuum cleaners, calculators, room robots, electric toothbrushes…you name it. There is an unofficial understanding among Marcus's relatives, neighbors, and classmates that if you have any kind of broken appliance, you should bring it to Marcus—not because he is a whiz at fixing them, but because he enjoys taking them apart and studying their components to see what he might be able to do with them or how he might be able to use them later in an invention or contraption of his own design. He loves figuring out how different machines work.

Melanie, a highly verbal fifth-grade student, carries a journal with her wherever she goes. She writes down interesting vocabulary she hears or snippets of conversations that grab her attention. These are her personal story starters, she says. She once wrote an entire short story around the word *magnificence*, and months later she wrote a poem of the same name.

Awareness often involves a strong sensory component. Our brains are wired to pick up considerable detail from the environment, and if we deliberately train, develop, and hone that capacity, the results can be amazing. One resource we've used successfully with children as young as five years and all the way up to graduate school level is Keri Ruef's book *The Private Eye: (5X) Looking/Thinking by Analogy*. That's a mouthful by itself, but now take a look at the subtitle, which is even longer but really describes what the book is about: *A Guide to Developing the Interdisciplinary Mind: Hands-On Thinking Skills, Creativity, Literacy, and Scientific Literacy.* Whew!

The projects in this book are all based on using a jeweler's loupe (a special magnifying device) to look closely at objects and other aspects of the environment. This process is layered with two analogical questions: "What does this look like?" and "What else does this remind me of?" The first exercise involves looking at one's thumbprint. Students view the end of their thumb through the jeweler's loupe, and then they draw their thumbprint with pencil on paper at a proportionately increased size. They visually represent just what they see, not an abstraction of what they think their thumbprint looks like. That way, the pressure of "drawing" is removed, and the emphasis is on representing or recreating the lines and "landmarks" (triangles, whorls, etc.) of the thumbprint as they see it. It is quite the adventure in observation.

The next step is to try to think of what the thumbprint looks like. Students' responses have included ocean currents as shown on a map, a sliced onion, rings in a tree trunk, ripples in the sand, a maze, vanilla fudge twirl ice cream, the Aurora Borealis, and even zebra stripes. Follow-ups to this activity might include writing a poem or short story or reflecting on the two-step seeing/imagining process.

But a thumbprint is just the beginning. We encourage you to help your child develop a mini-museum at home that could include rocks, seashells, dead bugs, dried plants or plant parts, small gears, samples of different styles of fabric, etc., all kept in a shoebox or similar container. Encourage your child to find and examine things and put those he considers special in his little museum-in-a-box. Then proceed with the jeweler's loupe activity, recreating the process of drawing the object on paper. In time, looking at things closely becomes second nature, and as one student said, "You realize that everything in the world has its own fingerprint!"

Talk about colors and textures when you look at paintings or shop for a new shower curtain. Sit outside at night when it's quiet and try to identify sounds you hear. Visit a home improvement store and look at the different kinds of wood and stone in the kitchen and bath displays, including the various kinds of granite and slate. Go hiking and try to locate the birds you hear singing in the trees above you.

Go outside and smell the air right before and then right after a rain shower. Make a game of trying to identify the various spices in a new dessert. Make an effort to be more aware of the many sights, sounds, smells, tastes, and textures of your surroundings, wherever you are. You are training your brain to notice things you didn't notice before.

Here are some questions to help children foster greater awareness and better observation:

- What is unique about this (object, color, shape, sound, smell, taste, texture)?
- Does this (object, color, shape, sound, smell, taste, texture) remind you of anything else? Is it similar? How? Different?
- How?
- What are its qualities?
- What are its parts and features?
- Can it be used for something new or different?

For an extra challenge, think of some favorite images in your mind's eye as if they were photographs. Can you describe your house or bedroom or best friend's face or…? Use as much detail as possible as you describe it.

Curiosity

With awareness comes curiosity. Once people become aware that things exist, they become curious about them. Curiosity involves wonder and possibility. Children are naturally curious and full of wonder. They wonder about how things are, why they are the way they are, how they might be or could be, and more. Creativity brings with it curiosity and abundant questions. At times, in our talks with parents and teachers, we have referred to this aspect of creativity as "The Perpetual Toddler Syndrome" because there is a phase between about two to three years of age when toddlers develop awareness of themselves as separate from their environment, want to understand as much about their surroundings as they can, and ask endless questions. Creative children—and adults—carry that habit with them throughout their lives. They ask:

- ❍ Why is ________ like that?
- ❍ What if I switched ________ with ________ to make a ________?
- ❍ What if we did ________ instead?
- ❍ What if we put ________ and ________ together?
- ❍ Do you ever wonder about ________? I do! What do *you* think about it?

In our schools today, thanks to the emphasis on standardized tests, finding the one right answer has taken priority over generating multiple possible responses formulated from multiple possible perspectives. Perhaps most disturbing is that answering questions is considered more important than generating one's own questions.

The Creativity/Curiosity Question Matrix in Table 3.2 offers an ideal starting point for creative writing assignments, research papers, invention projects, and more. The questions also can be used as prompts for opening class discussions, encouraging curiosity, and thinking about many possibilities, many ways of being curious, and many potential right answers instead of just one.

Table 5.2. Creativity/Curiosity Question Matrix

For	Who	What	When/ Where	Why	How
Investigation	Who is…?	What is….?	When/Where did…?	Why is…?	How is…?
Contemplation	Who can…?	What can…?	When/Where can…?	Why can…?	How can…?
Imagination	Who might…?	What might…?	When/Where might…?	Why might…?	How might…?

Parents may find the Creativity/Curiosity Question Matrix useful for helping their child generate ideas for further research or creative activity. For instance, parents might help the child with *investigation* of an area of interest by asking: Who were the originators of basketball?

What is the number of the most points earned by one player in a single game? When and where did basketball go from an informal game to a formalized game with rules and leagues?

Parents might support *contemplation* of a possible idea or project by asking: Who is allowed to hold a display of art or photography at the local bookstore or café? What are the limits on the subject matter? When and where might we plan trips to go through the neighborhood or the city to take pictures that you might want to display? How can you choose photos that will be artistic, unique, aesthetically pleasing, and vibrant so they will hold people's interest?

Further, parents can boost *imaginative* thought by discussing ideas for a story or a project:

- Who might be the main character for your story?
- What might be unusual or distinct about your character?
- When and where might your character live?
- Why would your character be motivated in your story?
- What would be his or her goals?
- How might your story progress and end on an exciting note?

Brainstorming

Sometimes children don't have ready answers to the questions adults may ask that are designed to get their creative juices flowing. What happens if a child feels stuck? What can people do when they can't seem to get out of the ruts of convergent thinking and need a bit of a push in the right direction?

Brainstorming is a terrific way to practice divergent thinking. It is a creative thinking approach that teachers and other leaders often use with groups. The purpose of brainstorming is to generate many different ideas, but there are some important guidelines to keep in mind during the process. Leaders should go over the guidelines with the group before starting the brainstorming session. The guidelines are:

1. *No criticism.* The specific term for this as it relates to brainstorming is *deferred judgment.* In other words, as ideas are generated, the rule is that no one blurts out a negative comment like "Oh, that's impossible," or "That will never work," or "Somebody already tried that," or "No one would

ever really *do* that!" To put it more simply, there are to be no put-downs of others' ideas and suggestions. This is important, because while one idea may not work, it may lead to another one that will. If criticism comes into play prematurely, it can—and usually will—shut down the creative process.

2. *Freewheeling is welcomed.* The wilder and more far-fetched the ideas, the better. People are more likely to find really creative ideas by going a bit wild first, then toning them down or refining them later. Again, no criticizing, evaluating, or editing as you go.

3. *Quantity is key.* The rationale behind generating as many ideas as possible is that the more ideas you have, the more likely it is that one of them will work.

4. *Combination and improvement are good.* When you start brainstorming with a group, and one person has an idea and then another person builds on it, that is called *hitchhiking*. When this happens in a group of children, sometimes the first child gets upset that the other "took" her idea. For example, let's say you are using a bamboo skewer as a brainstorming prop, and you ask, "What could this be used for?" Mia says, "It could be a pole vaulting pole for a mouse!" After hearing this, Brady pipes up, "It could be used for a mouse to dance the limbo, with that as the pole!" Indignant, Mia complains, "He took my idea!" That's a good time to discuss that hitchhiking (or piggybacking) on one another's ideas is a good thing; it's a form of creative collaboration. Brainstorming isn't a competition; it's a process to help us generate as many ideas as possible in a short amount of time.

Brainstorming is useful for coming up with solutions to problems, but it also can be an enjoyable activity on its own, and it's perfect for those "in-between times"—you know, when you have 10 minutes until dinner is ready, or your child has asked for the umpteenth time, "Are we there yet?" You might say, "Let's see how many ideas we can come up with. Let's brainstorm…":

- A list of things with stripes
- Things that are red
- Uses for old magazines
- Ways to show love
- Words related to fun
- Mythical creatures

The list goes on. You can think of more.

Some recent research has found that group brainstorming at the adult level in business settings does not produce more or better ideas than individuals working on their own and then pooling their ideas (Plucker, 2010). However, our experience in brainstorming with children is that they see it as a game, and it serves as a good warm-up or precursor for other creative pursuits.

Many people are familiar with the four elements that are commonly assessed in creativity exercises: fluency, flexibility, originality, and elaboration. Fluency is the ability to think of many ideas. Flexibility is the ability to think of many different kinds of ideas. Originality is the ability to think of unusual ideas. And elaboration is the ability to alter ideas, usually by adding to them, to make them better. Brainstorming can be a way to practice using all four of those elements, either simultaneously or by focusing on one at a time.

Fluency

Fluent thinking involves generating as many ideas as we can, and it is important to the creative process. When we have many possibilities to choose from, we have a better chance of finding an idea that will appeal to us or of finding a solution that will work. Fluency activities require that we search our background knowledge and breadth of experience to generate as many responses as possible. Thus, it makes sense that exposing children to many different kinds of experience can enhance their ability to be mentally and intellectually fluent.

Fluency also can be encouraged through games that require children (and adults) to be open-minded and creative in their responses—to think outside the box in order to produce more and more ideas for possible solutions to potential problems or novel answers to open-ended questions. Fluency games ask that an individual or a small group working together generate as many responses as possible to a given question or prompt. These may include questions such as:

- How many ________ can you think of? (e.g., things that are red, things that are round, animals that lay eggs, things that can be held in a juice glass, etc.)
- What are all the ways you could ________? (e.g., wash your hair, study for a test, send a message to a friend, celebrate a birthday, etc.)

As with any brainstorming technique, adults should insist that all ideas and answers be allowed without censorship; it is often the wildest ideas that lead to the most interesting creations, but it all starts with having a pile of ideas to select from, and this is something children can learn how to produce. Fluency games help children build these skills and are ideal for small-group work in classrooms or for family time in the car.

Flexibility

Flexibility is the ability to think of many different kinds of ideas. It is being able to look at things from different angles and to see situations from multiple perspectives. As with games that enhance children's ability to become more fluent, there are exercises that give children practice in being mentally flexible. One such creativity exercise involves giving children a page of same-size circles. The directions are to use the circles to make as many different things as they can think of by drawing or doodling with a pencil in or around the circles. When done in a group setting, the directions further state: "In the next 30 minutes, try to think of things no one else will think of."

A child who isn't used to thinking flexibly might complete all of the circles, but if he makes them all into a balls that are used in different sports (i.e., tennis, soccer, basketball, volleyball), that only demonstrates his ability to generate lots of ideas (fluency), but not his ability to be flexible in generating ideas. His thinking is stuck in a bit of a rut—he's not able to look at the potential of a circle from different perspectives. Alternatively, if he makes some of the circles into sports equipment, some into food items like apples and oranges and melons, some into eyes, a kitten curled up napping, a ladybug, a sun, and more, then he is demonstrating high fluency. Keep in mind that this exercise does not require great drawing skill; simple doodles are just as effective as elaborate drawings—maybe more so. The point is to get children thinking flexibly, since it has been shown that those who have greater flexibility in childhood tend to bring creativity into their adult pursuits (Czikszentmihalyi, 1997).

Elaboration

Elaboration is the creative thinking behavior of adding to or embellishing an idea. It is the ability to add details, fill in gaps, and expand concepts. A clear example of elaboration is jazz music. When various jazz musicians play together, one will start with a bit of a tune, and others will contribute harmonies or other embellishments on the theme.

A fun activity for improving or practicing one's elaboration skills is called "Creating a World in the Palm of Your Hand." This involves taking an old ball, or an inexpensive ball like those sold at discount stores, and creating a replica of the world on it with a combination of designed pieces and found objects. Materials could include:

- Construction paper
- Pipe cleaners
- Pieces of raffia
- Buttons and bits of fabric
- Objects from nature
- Nutshells or seashells as structures
- Gears, nuts, bolts, and other hardware store treasures

This is an activity that children and adults of all ages can enjoy. Creating a world becomes especially meaningful and even more imaginative when paired with a reading of Dr. Seuss's *Horton Hears a Who*, which is suitable for children of all ages, or Antoine de Saint Exupery's *The Little Prince*, for children in middle school or older. Both books describe the experience of visiting different worlds and connecting with their inhabitants.

Another way to practice elaboration is through collage. Choosing an initial image and then embellishing it with text, other pictures, or one's own writings or illustrations is a simple way to create an interesting piece of art. This technique also can be used to visually depict concepts from across subject areas, such as freedom, fusion, flight, ferries, faeries, and more.

Writing is often improved through elaboration as well. With a few adjectives and descriptive phrases, "The cat is sitting on the chair" becomes "The persnickety marmalade tabby-striped cat, Justina, is poised at the edge of the chair, ready to jump on Spot, her canine nemesis."

Writing

Since we're already discussing writing as it relates to elaboration, let's continue on that topic. Do you have a budding writer at your house? Perhaps your child cannot actually write yet but loves to make marks and tell stories. Perhaps she dictates her stories to her older siblings to write down for her. Or maybe she pecks away at a computer keyboard in a word processing program because it's the only way her hands can keep up with her ideas. Maybe she loves the feeling of pencil on paper, a half-filled journal on her lap as she contemplates how to resolve the latest crisis in her fantasy saga. If any of these sound familiar, we have two books that we highly recommend.

Jennifer Hallissy's book *The Write Start: A Guide to Nurturing Writing at Every Stage, from Scribbling to Forming Letters and Writing Stories* offers a unique take on the writing process (2010). The book includes 52 activities that can be adjusted for children ranging from early writers—the *scribblers*—to those whose scribbles have morphed into lines, shapes, drawings, and letters—the *spellers*—to those children, typically in the late primary or early intermediate grades, who are now writing multi-page stories—aptly called the *storytellers*—to those children who have moved beyond completely made-up stories to include research of various sorts—the *scholars.* Activities in the book include a travelogue; an Inventor's Logbook, complete with date stamp to validate authenticity; a "Once Upon a Time Book," which multiple family members can contribute to; and 49 more creative learning activities. One thing that makes Hallissy's book especially helpful is that she is a pediatric occupational therapist, so she includes lots of recommendations for parents of young children to help with pencil grip and good physical habits of writing.

The second book we recommend is Karen Benke's *Rip the Page! Adventures in Creative Writing (2010).* This book is best suited for children in middle school and beyond. It is filled to the brim with writing prompts, adventures that provide sources for stories, letters from other young writers, poems, and more. The introduction begins:

> *Dear Fellow Adventurer,*
>
> *Relax. This book isn't about assignments or homework or worksheets. This book is a not-so-secret combustible collection of ideas to excite and encourage the creative writer in you. It's a book for you to write in, explore, share, and rip—that's right, you get to tear the pages right out of this book! (But only if it's your book!) ....[Y]ou'll find Word Lists to help you when your writing is stuck, Try This experiments to spark new ideas, Suddenly a Story....*

And so the book continues in a friendly, welcoming, playful, and at times serious and emotional tone to provide encouragement for the budding creative writer to find his or her own voice, as well as reasons to write and express oneself.

Doodling, Drawing, Painting...

Creative people from across disciplines seem compelled to make marks. But not everyone who likes to put pencil to paper wants to write—some people prefer to draw instead. We prefer to use the word *doodle* rather than *draw*; the concept of drawing scares some people, as when people say, "I can't draw a straight line!" But that's okay! Straight lines are only one type of line, and in doodling, few lines are straight.

In our workshops with teachers and parents, we say, "Everyone can doodle!" Then we ask the participants to echo that phrase back to us. Often, it's a pretty half-hearted echo. So we'll ask that they amp up the volume and say it again with feeling. They still don't sound very convinced. However, when you work with a group of adults and bring out pencils and markers and crayons, give them big sheets of white paper, and provide a doodling prompt or two, how the spirit of the young child returns beautifully, and they doodle galore! Doodling is a fabulous creative warm-up activity. It's freeing! There's no way you can make a mistake or do it wrong.

We encourage you to make "doodle time" a regular part of your family's creative rituals. It's easy, it's quick, it requires few materials, and it can be done anywhere.

We also recommend two books. First is Ed Emberly's *Make a World* (2006), which illustrates how almost anything in the world can be visually created in a simple doodle-type style from just a handful of simple shapes. This is a children's book that we've recommended to scores of parents and teachers who have previously said, "I can't draw to save my life!" and who subsequently have experienced both great success and great enjoyment from the simple examples and methods in the book.

Another great resource for doodling, drawing, sketching, and painting is Carla Sonheim's *Drawing Lab for Mixed-Media Artists: 52 Creative Exercises to Make Drawing Fun* (2010). If you are one of those folks who feel that you can't draw, please don't be put off by the word *Drawing* in the title. This is a book meant for artists who *don't* draw—for instance, those who work in collage, fiber arts, modeling, crafting, and so on. It's simple and fun. The book includes, as its title suggests, 52 activities to tease out your inner doodler. The first activity is called "Draw Cats in Bed." Directions are as follows:

> Activity: *Draw about thirty cats from your imagination while sitting or lying in bed. If you are unsure where to start, go ahead and copy some of the cats on these pages.*
>
> *Or, better, spend some time just looking at a real cat before you begin.*
>
> Instructions: *(1) Gather your materials and get into bed. You can either sit up with your paper propped on a pillow, or lie on your stomach with the paper on the mattress. (2) Think about what a cat looks like: ears, face shape, body shape, tail, and*

just spend the next ten minutes or so drawing [DOODLING!] as many cats in as many positions as you can think of. (3) Try to keep your lines simple and expressive. If you find you are feeling tense, switch to your non-dominant hand. (4) Don't fret if you don't like many of your cats. It takes many drawings to get the "one" that you love.

There are a number of aspects of this activity that are creatively freeing. First, you get in bed! That immediately brings up the playful, out-of-the-ordinary, and definitely-not-serious aspects of this doodling activity. Then if you feel stuck, you switch to your non-dominant hand. This can be exceedingly frustrating at first, but it becomes liberating. If you are using your non-dominant hand, you can't expect your drawing to be "right," right?

Some of the other activities in Sonheim's book are:

- Imaginary Creatures
- Eyedropper Faces
- Picasso Dogs
- Your Inner Dr. Seuss
- Scribbly Drawings
- One-Eyed Monsters
- Machines and Inventions

- Drawing Out Your Passions
- Exploring Story: Illustrating Fairy Tales

Some of these activities bring in other media, like paint and collage elements. A few of them use paint as a starting point, in which you make different kinds of paint blotches and work those into a more elaborate design. And imagine this: There are 42 more activities beyond these! It is truly a great resource that encourages parents and children to co-create and have a good time together. Art and doodling are freeing activities. When you decide to try some of the ideas, politely ask your inner critic to take a coffee break, and then roll up your sleeves to explore and play with your child. We're pretty confident you'll both want to do it again!

Creative Dramatics

Creative dramatics are another great way to foster creativity in children. There is a story featuring the acclaimed actress Lucille Ball that we want to share here.

After Lucille died in 1989, her daughter, Lucy Arnez, narrated a documentary of her mother's life. As part of the documentary, Lucy conducted a tour of the childhood house where Lucille Ball grew up. The house had a large entry hall followed by three doorways that went to different parts of the house. In one of the doorways was a curtain so that every night after dinner, Lucille could perform for her family. Sometimes those performances were planned, and sometimes they were spontaneous. Sometimes neighbors would even come over for an evening performance. The documentary does not mention whether anyone in the family before Lucille had acting experience or talent, but the presence of the curtain surely indicates that Lucille's parents knew how to foster their daughter's talent. In addition, this is clearly an example of how Lucille's creative dramatics progressed from mini-c to little-c to Pro-c to Big-C creativity, with support all along the way.

Creative dramatics activities are easy to encourage—whether or not you have prior acting experience. Just getting some old scarves, hats, purses, a cane, or other props from a closet or an old trunk in an attic can be the start of an afternoon or evening performance. Creative drama runs the gamut from a simple game of "statues" to a full staging of an original one-act play. The important thing is to encourage the children to be creative in their acting and productions. Pantomime warm-ups and pantomime stories are a simple way to start.

Pantomime warm-ups include:

- *Circles*: A group of children or a parent and child, in turn, think of a way to make a circle by using his or her body. Other players then make the same circle. The circle can be made with part of the body or all of the body; it can be a fixed circle or a moving circle, such as a circular motion of the foot or rolling on the floor. Names can add to the fun: "This is a halo circle," "This is an eyeball circle," or "This is a chicken walking in a circle."
- *Mirrors*: This activity requires two people facing each other. One person acts as the "mirror" and copies or mimics the motions of the other, who may be combing hair, making faces, or doing ballet—all very slowly. After a few minutes, the partners switch, and the one copying becomes the one who initiates the action.
- *Obstacles*: With chalk, draw a "start" line and a "finish" line about eight feet apart from each other. One at a time, each player makes up an imaginary obstacle that must be climbed over, dodged past, waded through, or overcome in some other way to get from start to finish. Players must "describe" the obstacle with their bodies—to indicate, for example, a fence, a puddle, a gate, stepping stones, or a fallen log across a creek. Others must guess what the obstacle is.
- *Nature's shapes*: Children shape their bodies to become a tree, stone, leaf, growing flower, rain, sun, etc. The others must guess what they are pretending to be. Pantomime stories include:
  - *Who Am I? (Who Are We)?* Children act out the roles of community helpers—teachers, firefighters, nurses, doctors, historical or literary characters, or characters from movies

or television. Classmates or others in the group guess who they are portraying.

- *What Am I (What Are We)?* Children act as animals, plants, inanimate objects, machinery, toys, or mythical creatures. The possibilities are endless. Again, classmates or others in the group try to guess who or what they are.
- *What Am I (What Are We) Seeing/Hearing/Smelling/Tasting/ Touching?* Children mime reacting to a loud sound, tasting a bitter fruit, smelling strong fumes, touching a hot stove, and so on. They could peel and eat a banana, hear a helicopter overhead, taste a lemon, see a car chase, touch something hot. The others guess what they're doing or experiencing.
- *Where Am I (Where Are We)?* Children mime being in various locations, such as at a museum, on a boat, in a foreign land, or on a spaceship. They could act as if they were paddling a kayak or climbing a mountain. As before, the other children guess where they are and what they're doing.

❍ *Inventions:* Children can mime either using a tool or actually being an invention—for example, wearing a snorkel while swimming, using a metal detector to make an exciting find, or being a robot serving beverages to a group of people.

❍ *Musical instruments:* Children act out playing a musical instrument of their choice or one from a category, such as orchestral, marching band, percussion, woodwind, or brass. They might pretend to play one or more drums, a piano, a trombone, a flute, etc.

❍ *Countries and customs:* Children enact a custom or celebration associated with a particular country or culture, such as eating with their hands while sitting on the floor, serving high tea, maneuvering at a bullfight, doing an ethnic dance, or performing a coronation.

Dan had an opportunity to experience what children can do with creative dramatics when they put their minds to it. His three children and five of his nieces and nephews, all between the ages of eight and 18, spent a week producing a short silent film. Set in the Roaring '20s, it is the story of a woman who is taken by kidnappers who try to ransom her for money, but her friends outwit the bad guys and rescue her to save the day. The eight youngsters not only wrote the film and created the costumes, but they did it all in the classic style of the silent film era. They raided their grandmother's dress-up chest for period dresses, hats, and high heels. They used sections of the house that contained antiques for their settings. And significantly, they did it all in black and white, using old-style music and written dialogue to explain the plot, just like the silent films of yesteryear. The children spend days on the script, making sure to include suspense, emotion, and the battle between good and evil. Then came filming, with take after take to get it just right. Next, editing and post-production, during which they added dramatic elements like a replay of the primary action scene in slow motion. Together, the team agreed upon font, music, and scenes. Finally, they posted the finished product on YouTube for all to see. Making it relevant to the times, they even added a "Bloopers" section in color at the end, showing the fun they had along the way. Wow!

Not every child will attack dramatic pursuits with such gusto, but even lesser forms of drama, such as pantomime stories, skit activities using improvisation, and reader's theater that uses a script for the characters, will help children build their divergent thinking abilities and will give them an alternate outlet for creative expression.

SCAMPER

SCAMPER is an idea-generating technique. Similar to elaboration, it is based on the notion of mentally making changes to objects in your surroundings to create something new, or at least a novel variation of something that already exists. SCAMPER stands for:

- **S**ubstitute
- **C**ombine
- **A**dapt

- **M**inify, magnify, modify
- **P**ut to other uses
- **E**liminate
- **R**everse or rearrange

So to SCAMPER or generate ideas about an Oreo cookie, for example, you might *substitute* mint filling, *combine* it with ice cream, *adapt* it by making smaller snack packages rather than an entire box, *magnify* or *minify* it by making each cookie larger or smaller or even putting in double the filling, *put it to other uses* by creating an Oreo-shaped keychain, *eliminate* by changing the recipe to create low-fat Oreos; and *reverse* or *rearrange* it by making three layers of cookie and two of frosting.

Now, as anyone who loves Oreos knows, most of these variations already have been created over the past decade or so. But once upon a time, there was just the plain, original Oreo in the cookie aisle of the grocery store. Someone at the Nabisco company had to come up with the ideas for these new kinds of Oreos, and one can imagine that the SCAMPER method might have been pretty useful in that context.

What other items might you SCAMPER to make new or interesting variations? A bicycle? A highlighting pen? A mug? A rowboat? A computer mouse?

Children's "Toolbox"

Kids love *stuff*! Paper, pencils, cardboard, straws, aluminum foil, crayons, paints, glue, scissors, and tape! We have seen some spectacular tape sculptures—to say nothing of the many aluminum foil creations over our years of working with children! How often is it that a child enjoys the packing materials that a mailed item comes in at least as much as the item itself? Raw materials such as a large cardboard box can provide hours of fun and inspiration. (We know of one preschool that asked parents to donate large and small packing boxes so the students could create and then paint an entire cardboard city.) It is also good for children, even very young children, to spend time using tools and equipment from various fields—painting, wood-crafting, sewing, cooking, science, and more.

Adults can help foster creativity in children by helping them make a special "toolbox" of items that the youngsters can use to create with, whether by making an artistic collage, building a machine, or discovering similarities among different kinds of plants, insects, and animals. If they have access to the materials and equipment, the wheels in their minds will churn with ways to use them, and they'll be building their capacity for creative imagining and production in the process. Children love to make things with objects and tools like those listed in Table 3.3.

Table 5.3. Objects for Your Child's Toolbox

Houschold and Repurposed Objects	**Tools**
• Cardboard tubes • Popsicle sticks • Packing materials • Aluminum foil • Boxes • Cookie cutters • Spatulas • Bowls • Pans	• Pliers • Screw drivers—flat and Phillips • Wrench • Hammer • Goggles • Safety saw • Protractor • Compass • Level
Art	**Science**
• Newsprint • Colored pencils • Cardstock or file folders • Adhesive tape, duct tape • Chalk, crayons, markers, pens • White paper and colored paper • Watercolors • Glue • Embellishments, sequins, etc. • Needles and thread • Fabric scraps • Sewing machine	• Magnifying glass • Magnifying boxes • Tweezers • Dried plants and wood • Flower press • Bug and small mammal skeletons • Broken machines to take apart • Graduated beakers • Terrarium • Pulleys, screws, nuts, and bolts • Museum-in-a-box (from the wareness section of this chapter)

Parents and teachers who are open to allowing their children to experiment with these types of materials and, yes, to make a mess are to be applauded. Plan ahead for the occasional mess by putting plastic over anything you want protected, or set up a workshop outside.

Boosting Creative Potential with Games and Playful Activities

As you can see, there are many activities and games that you can do with children—exercises that a child can do individually or that you can do as a family or in a classroom—to exercise and strengthen their divergent thinking skills (as well as your own).

Remember, this chapter is meant to serve as a resource and activity guide, not as homework or a step-by step "how to" guide. Try one of these activities on a rainy day, when things are "boring," when you want some parent-child bonding time, or when your classroom students need a creative boost. Most importantly, have fun, and let your imagination run wild!

Chapter 6
Creative Projects for the Whole Family

The family home is often the canvas, studio, lab, springboard, and space where the seeds of creativity begin and where creativity is nurtured and supported. In this space, creativity can take form in both quiet and energetic moments, as well as occur alone or with others. The family and the family home provide opportunities for engagement and collaboration, while learning the important life skills of flexibility, negotiation, and compromise—while being creative and having fun. The following are examples of family projects that include food, nature, entrepreneurism, and exploration to enhance creativity and positive family memories.

Family Garden

The family garden can take many forms depending on one's space, geography, and climate. Creating a family garden starts with a conversation about how much space is available for the garden, the season or seasons one is able to plant depending on your climate, the types of vegetables, fruit, herbs, and flowers one would like to plant, and the type of irrigation system.

> **Space**—Depending on the amount of space on has (an apartment with a balcony or small enclosed space, backyard, or larger rural land), the garden can be designed to fit the space ranging from a planter box, half barrel(s), or metal feeding trough, to a 10 ft. x 10 ft. plot in the yard, to a much larger designated area.
>
> **Climate**—One's geography will determine the seasons one can have a garden. Colder places will likely only allow for growth in the spring whereas warmer regions will also allow for winter gardens. Having multiple garden seasons will allow for more variety of vegetation.
>
> **Vegetation**—One's climate will also determine what one can grow, or at least what grows best. Family members can research the different types of vegetation options for the area.
>
> **Irrigation**—There are many types of irrigation including a watering can, hose, or setting up a drip system. The type of system will depend upon the size of the garden, what works best for the family, the budget, and the desire to have, and learn about designing, an irrigation system.

The family garden starts with a discussion about all of the items above. With creative kids, the family garden plan often starts in an expansive form—large, and with many types of vegetation. As is often the case with creative kids, it is a delicate balance of supporting their ideas while bringing reality into the discussion about what is possible for your space, climate, and budget.

Some simple guiding questions are:

- ❍ What plants (vegetables, fruits, and herbs) grow well in our area?
- ❍ What type of garden should we have (raised bed or in the ground)?
- ❍ What do you want to grow?
- ❍ How will we water the garden?
- ❍ When (what month) do we plant?
- ❍ How much work do we need to do prior to planting?
- ❍ What is our budget?

The family garden discussions can take place on a few occasions as you may be able to answer all the questions together and look up the information together. With older kids you may assign different information gathering tasks to different family members. A meeting can then be set to share what each found and come up with a family garden plan.

Let's take the example of the Phan family, who are parents (Vanessa and Don) and two kids (Sabrina, age 8 and Dax, age 6). During their meeting about their family garden, they talked about the topics above and were able to teach their kids that they have an option for one Spring garden since they live in the Midwest, have enough room for an approximately 8 ft x 8 ft garden in their backyard, and would take turns watering with a hose. Dax was excited to grow a peppers and flowers, and Sabrina wants to grow strawberries and tomatoes. They each were given a budget of $40 so they would need to decide on the amount and type of plants. They then discussed what they needed to do to prepare the ground to be ready to plant in April or May. Finally, they determined a watering schedule.

The kids couldn't wait for their plants to grow, checking on them every morning and afternoon. This was definitely an exercise in patience as they had to wait for the plants to sprout and take form. Then came the question of when to pick them or let them grow and experimenting with that timing. The family all felt a sense of responsibility for the garden and experienced joint disappointment when some plants didn't grow and delight when eating organic vegetables that they grew on their own. At the end of the season, they discussed what worked, what they learned, and what they wanted to do next year.

Garage Sales

Family garage sales provide an opportunity to recycle clothes, games, and toys, and learn about money, and business. Garage sales also provide an experience for kids to be able to part with objects they are connected to, but no longer use and need, in order for others to derive joy and use from them. Similar to the family garden, the family garage sale starts with a discussion about the idea of having a garage sale, the purpose, and how each family member with participate.

Questions to ask:

- ❍ What are things (items, toys, games, clothes) we don't need anymore?
- ❍ Of those items, what do we care about, and what do we not care about?
- ❍ What toys/items are you ready to let go of so others can find joy in them?
- ❍ What items do you want to sell and what do you want to give away for free?
- ❍ How do you want to set up your selling space?
- ❍ How will we let people know about our family garage sale?
- ❍ What kind of signs do we want to make and where should we put them?

Just like planning for the family garden, the family garage sale may take a few conversations to determine the items, arrange the sale space, and plan the signs and their neighborhood distribution. Considerations for the timing of the sale include weather and a family's readiness and motivation to go from idea to sale.

Rhonda, mother of Josiah, age 10, and Layla, age 12, brought the idea of a garage sale to her kids. She said it was time for getting rid of extra items and objects they no longer needed, as well as an opportunity to create space, and make money. The kids were excited about the idea of making some money and Rhonda was excited about the proposition of more space and less stuff in the house and her storage closets.

They decided that they would each go through their own rooms and make a pile of everything they wanted to sell. Then they went through the house together and each asked the others if different items were still used and needed. Although Rhonda had the final decision, she found it helpful to hear about her kids' ideas concerning what they found useful or irrelevant, which allowed her to reconsider some of her beliefs about what "stuff" was important, or not so important.

Once they determined they had enough items for a sale, they looked at the weather forecast and their family calendar to determine the day of the sale. After some discussion, they agreed on how many big signs they needed and where to place them, and how many small signs to post around the neighborhood. They then bought poster boards and colored paper to make signs. Excited to sell their items, and make money, they then put prices on each item with tape. Rhonda then told them about all prices being "negotiable" and how to engage with buyers who ask to pay less. She told them this is part of the culture of garage sales and also part of the fun—seeing how much you can get for your item, while still making a sale. She educated them about getting something is better than getting nothing. They also agreed that they would donate all of the items that were left after the sale.

Garage sale day came after putting out all the flyers and telling all of their friends. They experienced the frustration of people looking and not buying anything, many people asking them questions at once, negotiating, and ultimately counting money and change. After the sale, they bagged up the leftover items for donation, felt a sense of satisfaction with their new-found space, and talked about what they were going to do with the money they made.

Family Adventures

The family adventure has endless possibilities and can be implemented in a few different ways. The family adventure can be of no to low cost to more costly, from going to state parks and tide pools, to natural springs and the beach, to the zoo or Disneyland. Family adventures are meant to create excitement about going someplace unknown, new, or a place that brings the family joy. The family adventure was an important part of Dan's family when his kids were young, and the adventures are still talked about years later. One way of doing the family adventure is when the parents pick the adventure. This is usually the way it is done with young kids. As the kids get older, they can be a part of the planning, by taking turns with each child getting to plan an "adventure." This allows for each child to organize an adventure that pertains to their own interest (that the other family members may or may not share), and gives an opportunity for other family members to engage in the adventure with respect and an open mind, as each member knows they will have a turn planning an adventure for the others.

Questions to ask:

- ❍ Would you like to start a family adventure activity in the family where each person gets to plan an entire day on the weekend?
- ❍ What are some of your ideas for a family adventure?
- ❍ Can everyone agree that they will accept and engage in the family adventure even if it is not what they would have chosen?
- ❍ Do you think you can plan an adventure if you are given a budget of X dollars?

Parents generally find that kids have a difficult time understanding how much adventures can cost. This is a great way to teach about finances and budgets. As with the family garden, you will find your creative kids planning elaborate (and expensive!) family adventures. Again, the key is to work with them to plan an adventure that fits in the budget while still allowing for creativity and adventure in an affordable and doable way. Steps include setting a budget, choosing the frequency (such as once a month), and deciding on the order of adventure planners.

The Lopez family of five has three teens, Jesus, age 16, Serena, age 14, and Gorge, age 13. They each have varied interests, yet all agreed to be open minded about the others adventure. Jesus loves baseball. His adventure included going to a baseball game with a barbeque in the parking lot prior to the game, and then his favorite home cooked meal after at home. Serena loves the theatre. Her adventure included a day in the city and then going to a musical. Gorge loves art, and to his sibling's chagrin, chose a day of modern art museums and seeing the work of local artists. Each family member looked forward to their planned adventures, and tolerated, to varying degrees, their sibling's adventures. Most of the time, they each liked the other's adventure more than they had thought they would.

Camping—Home and Away

Another favorite of Dan's family when his kids were young was the family campout. Excitement ensued when the kids knew they were going to get to sleep in front of the fire in the family room. The goal was to create a different experience in a usual space. They would push all of the furniture to the edges of the room and lay down sleeping bags. This family activity triggered imagination, as the home was transformed into the outdoors. The kids would choose popcorn or s'mores, and often both. Negotiations occurred about who would sleep next to who and which stuffed animals (also known as "Stuffies") would come camping with them. The family dog would also come on the adventure. All lights were turned off and all would watch the shadows of the fire on the walls and ceiling. A family bedtime story or two topped off the evening.

For older kids, the home campout can move to the backyard, terrace, or balcony. Choices, for discussion, include whether to sleep in a tent or under the stars, whether to BBQ or cook inside, and whether parents camp out with the kids, or the kids do it alone (with parents inside). Stories (or camp-fire stories), read or made up on the spot, add to the camping experience.

And then there is camping in the great outdoors. Some may be wondering why camping is considered a creative activity. The reason is that camping occurs in nature, and being in nature is often credited with sparking ones creativity, imagination, and innovation. Many of the most creative minds in music, science, and politics talk about the importance of their daily walks in nature. Going camping not only allows kids to learn how to plan, prepare, and help with set up and cooking at the camp site; it allows time for exploration, introspection, and to gaze up at the vast expanse of the universe while watching for shooting stars and identifying constellations. Because many of our creative kids are deep thinkers, peering up at the universe can promote family conversations about our place in the universe, time, and existence. Key in these conversations is to allow for everyone's point of view to be heard and respected.

Holiday and Birthday Celebrations

Holiday and birthday celebrations allow an excellent opportunity for creativity and ritual. Children love contributing to the decorations, from making signs and banners, to setting the table and helping with cooking. A birthday ritual in Dan's family, which was greatly anticipated, was picking the pinata. Each child got to pick the one for their birthday party, while receiving input (which was not always accepted) from their siblings. Other rituals include the types of foods and who cooks them. For example, mashed potatoes for Thanksgiving, latkes for Hannukah, and sheppard's pie for Christmas.

While it is common for adults to do the planning and want to do the work themselves to "get it done," involving kids in the process is not only a wonderful opportunity to help them feel a part of the celebration, it also to allows them to form ideas about how they would like to contribute. Their ideas are their creative process at play.

Questions to ask:

- ❍ What do you think we should do this year for....?
- ❍ I know we always do X for Mom's birthday, what do you think we should do this year?

- ❍ What would you like to make for our holiday celebration? How do you want to contribute?
- ❍ How do you think we should decorate for the party this year?
- ❍ Do you think we should have a theme? If so, what do you think it should be?

Family Business, e.g., Lemonade Stand

More and more kids, and families, are starting legitimate businesses with the help of technology and social media these days. Family businesses range from good ol' lemonade stands to on-line clothing businesses to starting non-profits. Any sort of business idea, small or large, allows for creativity in the form of planning, problem-solving, and implementation. It also provides a wonderful opportunity for having to be patient, dealing with frustration, being flexible, and growing resilience. because things don't always work or turn out the way we want on the first try. Welcome to the world of entrepreneurs!

Dan's son began his foray into the entrepreneurial world with a lemonade stand. His drive was to make money from a giant lemon bush in the yard that produced a ton of lemons. This "business" started with several questions:

- ❍ How much money can I make from a lemonade stand?
- ❍ Where is the best place to have it?
- ❍ What do I need to do it?
- ❍ How long will it take?
- ❍ How do I make lemonade?
- ❍ How can we let people know?

He quickly learned this was a slower process than he thought from picking the lemons, to squeezing them, to making a mixture that tasted good, to setting up the table, to making signs, to sitting and waiting for customers. The first experience led to improvements at lemon picking (gloves to prevent being cut by the spikes), new locations, and a new work force; he hired his friends to work the stand while he managed the production. This experience also led to researching juice squeezers and an attempt to design his own.

The lemonade stand is a classic example of learning about business, but as mentioned, there are tons of ways these days for children and adolescents to start a business such as selling and reselling shoes and clothes, Legos, and more. We must remember that some of our most creative minds express their creativity through business and it's never too early to cultivate creative business thinking in your child. They key is to support your child's creative ideas while initially not telling them why it can't be done or is too complicated, which puts a damper on the creative spirit and creative risk taking. Instead, engage in, and guide, exploration of their ideas so they can see the possibilities, as well as where they may need to change or alter their ideas. Remember, it is about the creative process and keeping your child engaged in the process of discovery.

Family Meals

All families have meals, so this is a great opportunity to get their kids, and their creative ideas, involved in the process. Some families cook together, others, depending on the age of the child, have children take turns cooking meals. Cooking is not only an opportunity for learning an important life task, but also for taking risks while trying new ingredients and creations.

When inviting your child to cook with you, it is important to be aware of your own cooking style and temperament. Do you follow the recipe to the letter? Do you make it up as you go? Are you somewhere in between? There is no right or wrong way of course, rather it is important to know what behavior you will be modeling for your child so you can see if this fits your child's approach, or if they are inclined to do it differently. As parents we want both to teach them how we do things *our* way, and at the same time support them in finding *their* way.

Questions to ask:

- ❍ What should we make for dinner tonight (or this week)?
- ❍ What do you want to make?
- ❍ Do you want help or to do to it by yourself?
- ❍ What ingredients do you think you will need?
- ❍ Do you want to follow a recipe or do it your own way?

- How do you think it turned out?
- Would you make this again? Would you change anything?

Boosting Your Family's Natural Creativity

It is important to support our kids' development by positively reinforcing their efforts and behavior, yet we must also be mindful to let them have their own thoughts and feelings and not just rely on *our* responses to them to determine how they did. We want them to have their *own* thoughts and feelings about what they do that is separate from us and others. This helps develop a strong internal sense of themselves. Thus, the family meal allows for experiences of independence, creativity, and internal growth.

As you can see, there are many different kinds of family projects that promote creativity and teach important life skills of risk taking, planning, collaboration, negotiation, and problem-solving. Family projects also allow for family connection and the creation of family rituals and memories. Creativity is a part of every family. You just have to be aware of it, look for it, and cultivate it. Fostering creativity in the context of your home is not only good for your child's development, it can be great fun as well.

CHAPTER 7
Creative Spaces—Welcome Home!

Wherever you go, there you are!

~ Unknown

As we discussed in Chapter 1, the creative press is one of the four P's of creativity. The word *press* here means the influence of the environment—of place and space. Your family environment can help to encourage and support creativity, or it can do just the opposite.

As we talk about the family environment in this chapter, we will discuss creativity in the home, taking into account much more than just the physical environment. The quote above, *Wherever you go, there you are,* is less about location and more about mindfulness which might not be clear from a cursory reading. When we apply the concept to families, we can assume the same conclusion: When you take your family out and about, you take your family environment with you. Your family environment includes attitudes, behaviors, dynamics, and habits, as much as it does sofas, tables, books, beds, and perhaps a tree house in the backyard.

Creative Space: A Playful Family Environment

Teresa Amabile, who is now an endowed Professor of Entrepreneurial Management at Harvard's Business School, wrote *Growing Up Creative* after spending much of her early career studying, observing, working with, and interviewing creative children and their families. Amabile's advice to parents is to:[45]

> *Play with your kids; especially, quit instructing them. Just go with them. Let them tell you what things are about instead of you always telling them, because they see things in a totally different, sometimes bizarre, sometimes wonderful way.*

She vividly describes her experience of visiting the home of one child, Jason, whom she interviewed along with his family. A playwright at age 12, Jason lived in a complex and ever-evolving creation that was his family home. Amabile described it this way:[46]

> *From the outside, the Brown-Cohen house seems rather ordinary. But inside, it is quite remarkable, filled with unusual objects. Here is my partial list of what I saw throughout the house: six typewriters (old, but still working); two computers; a piano; a pool table; a neon sign saying "OOPS"; photographs everywhere (including dozens of old family photographs); an electric piano; dozens of board games; hundreds of books; an unfinished wood door to the family room that has been carved with the children's graffiti (examples: "Homework Stinks" rendered in several different styles, drawings of fantastic characters, "Abandon all hope, ye who enter here"); false teeth ice tongs in the kitchen, art prints on the walls in every room;*

oil paintings by Carol [Jason's mother]; a guitar belonging to Jeffrey [Jason's father]; a variety of bizarre postcards plastered on the bathroom wall; in the formal dining room, a framed painting done by one of Jason's brothers in first grade; in the kitchen, a satirical essay written by another brother on "How To Be A Good Kid"; a poster in the kitchen saying "Avenge yourself: live long enough to be a problem to your children"; a light sculpture and a pin-art sculpture in the living room; stickers all over one bedroom door; on another bedroom door, a beautifully lettered poster saying "The Wretched Hive of Scum and Villainy"; two dogs; two cats; four hermit crabs; a fish; a lizard; and twelve snakes.

Wow! Amabile went on to wonder what sort of message this style of home gave to the children. There was definitely an atmosphere of freedom in the house—as shown by the "Homework Stinks" door graffiti, the "Avenge yourself" poster, the collection of postcards glued to the bathroom wall, the variety of musical instruments and artworks and animals, and the many other unusual artifacts scattered throughout the home. There were many options for engagement and for nourishing a wide range of interests in this house. In fact, when Jason was three, he slept for several months in a refrigerator box he had decorated and in which he had put a small mattress. When a child grows up in such a house, he will no doubt absorb a message that the possibilities for experiences and experiments are endless.

Think about your own home environment. What adorns your walls? Are there spaces that are set aside for creating and imagining? Are there areas that are off limits to children? Does your house lean more toward being cluttered with stuff, or is it more open and spacious? There is no right or wrong answer to any of these questions. The point to keep in mind is that your home and the space in and around it is your child's creative playground. As such, we recommend giving your child some space and some creative fodder to explore both his inner and outer worlds.

Creative Zones

If you're living in an austere house that suddenly seems a little bit plain or minimalistic, don't worry. A house as unusual as the Brown-Cohen's is not an absolute necessity for fostering creativity in children at home. Families of children we've worked with often describe "creative zones" in their homes. While it's fine to build a cardboard fort in the living room or to stretch a sheet over some dining room chairs to make a cave, sometimes those areas are needed for other purposes (like entertaining or dining). When a fort right in the center of the main living space isn't practical, parents can establish areas in the house or "zones" that are designed and used specifically for creative activity.

As we write this, we wonder how many of our adult readers have a woodshop, an art studio, a "man cave" in the basement, or a craft space in that extra room over the garage. Children, whose work and play intermingle, respond well to art centers, science labs, building spaces, tree houses, and even little studios in the basement or garage. More than a few families we know have built small cottages in the backyard that are creative zones where their children can have a place for daydreaming and reverie or design and construction, where materials are always at hand, and where their mess-making won't affect the rest of the house. Creating such a space can be a creative activity unto itself.

Many a garage has been set up as a science lab or a robotics shop. A garage or basement or screened-in porch works well for making large works of art or performing original plays. One family we work with has had a collaborative family mural in process in the garage for more than a year. Incorporating all sorts of mixed media—including paint, chalk, yarn, buttons, a Barbie doll, photos from family excursions, poetry, quotes, pictures from magazines, messages to one another, wrapping paper and ribbon from holidays and parties, and more—this mural is an evolving work of art, as well as a record of the year's activities.

We know another family that has two children and that lives in a small flat in a big city. Their children's creative zones are tucked under their beds in plastic crates—long, thin boxes that house the current project under construction. Each child has his or her own creative crate that can be pulled out and taken to the dining room table, the living room floor, or even the balcony of the apartment in good weather. Rather than seeing their lack of space as an obstacle to creative potential, these family members view their circumstances as simply requiring flexibility and adaptability, which themselves are keys to creative development.

Plenty of folks have similar issues with a lack of space, but a little bit of creative thinking can turn even hallways into creative zones. Still another family we know lives in a tiny cottage of a home, but they have a roll of butcher paper hanging at one end of a hallway that leads out to the backyard. The hallway serves as a "family museum" space with ever-changing exhibits, and a covered porch just outside the back door contains cubbies and tubs filled with myriad art and science materials. The best part is that all messy projects can be cleaned up with a good spray from the garden hose.

> *A few years ago, the Tolliver family added a detached garage to their home. More importantly, they added a small music/art room at the back of the garage. This room is now known as the "art room," including a drum set, guitar, and amplifiers set up at one end. The children's art hangs on every wall. Visitors to the art room will find an endless supply of colored paper, pens, all types of paints, brushes, beads, glue, tape, and more. There is a large worktable splattered with paint and glue stains, and it is surrounded by stools. There is a small sign on the wall by the light switch with a quote from Pablo Picasso that says, "If you know exactly what you are going to do, what's the point of doing it?"*
>
> *When Mrs. Tolliver can't find one or more of her three children, she goes to the art room, as there is a very good chance that at least one of them is there. They go there when they need to make a project for school or a gift for a friend, when they are upset, or just to create and see what happens. Some projects reach completion, while others lie quietly waiting, in process, maybe to be completed one day but maybe not. The art room is also the gathering space when the cousins come to town. The*

cousins cherish the time being in that room—taking chances with their art, giving each other ideas and feedback, and creating as a family.

Attitude

Teresa Amabile also found that attitude is a key component for parents who want to encourage and facilitate creativity in their children. A supportive attitude consists of the interplay between acceptance, mutual respect, and flexibility. Parents of creative children provide them with considerable freedom within limits. For example, they may say, "You may make things or paint to your heart's content in this workspace with the tile floor, but those arts and crafts need to stay in this area for easy cleanup later." These parents communicate respect for their children, are emotionally close and connected but not overly so, and focus on values rather than rules, and achievement over grades.

In her work, Amabile discovered that the parents of creative children have other similarities. They tend to be independent and active, hold a deep appreciation for creativity, have a vision for their child's growth and development that includes considerable exploration, and maintain a sense of humor—even in the face of what others might consider quite trying circumstances. Many of the parents are involved in mini-c or little-c pursuits themselves, and some are engaged at the Pro-c level.

Time Out

In *Living with Intensity,* a book about the social and emotional development of gifted and creative children, youth, and adults, the concept of children taking a "time out" is presented as a personal choice rather than a punishment. Most people are familiar with parents using "time out" as a way of reprimanding children for bad behavior. However, sometimes children need to request "time outs" of their own. Although creative kids tend to enjoy a wealth of activity or deep immersion in an area of interest, quiet time is also essential for them to refuel their creative spirit. We highly recommend unscheduled, unplanned time for children—and their parents—to simply relax and regenerate. This is good for everyone's overall health and well-being, and it facilitates the opportunity for the incubation described in the Wallas model of creativity discussed in Chapter 2.

This chapter opened with a quote, "Wherever you go, there you are," which is also the title of a book by Jon Kabat-Zinn published in 1994. He is the man responsible for bringing mindfulness practices—essentially breath-centered meditation—to hospitals in the United States in the 1990s as a form of complementary medicine, first with cardiac patients and then with a wider variety of patients and clients, from cancer patients to expectant parents. In April 2012, Kabat-Zinn gave a talk at the University of California at Berkeley on *mindful schools*. These are schools that are using mindfulness practices to lower student anxiety, build calmness and community as part of the classroom environment and culture, and help students relax and focus as a way to promote better learning and development. Even simple breathing practices (such as breathing in to the count of four, holding for a count of four, exhaling to the count of four, and holding for a count of four) can lower anxiety and increase creative responses to classroom activities. These easy activities provide an opportunity to filter out extraneous sounds and visual stimuli and gain a moment of quiet within—a moment to focus on oneself and re-center during the bustle of the day.

Periods of quiet, rest, and alone time are essential to creativity. In fact, in the fascinating book *Cradles of Eminence*,[47] which studies the childhoods of more than 700 eminently creative and inventive people, a common theme is that these individuals needed lots of alone time—time to be with their own thoughts, ideas, inventions, and creations. We of course are not suggesting that you neglect your child, but we do want to emphasize that alone time is a key aspect of being creative.

Time In

"Time in" is a notion that we use to describe days or "dates" at home—making a conscious decision to set aside a day, usually a Saturday or Sunday, to hang out at the house and do something creative. Some parents we know even schedule one day off from school each quarter for their child for this purpose. It's a day to stay home, relax, and do something special—maybe make a special food or pursue a special activity. In our highly scheduled society, "time in" can be treasured time. It could be a day when the whole family decides to work on the plans for the cottage in the backyard, or perhaps each family member has his or her own project or activity to pursue. This family "parallel play" may then converge at a nice lunch, during which all come together and share updates on their activities. The evening might include another round of "progress reports" on each family member's activity, or perhaps someone might read aloud, or several members might write in a family journal, documenting the specialness of the day.

Sometimes these creative "time in" dates can go on for days, possibly over a holiday or summer vacation. Remember the kids we discussed earlier in the book who spent a week producing a silent film? That was a terrific example of "time in." In fact, those same children spend every holiday producing a new Christmas play for their entire extended family (which amounts to about 75 people!). Whether children use their "time in" for individual projects or collaborative ones, setting aside dedicated time to work on projects of their choosing is an excellent way to nurture their creative spirits.

Right in Your Own Backyard—Nature and the Creative Spirit

It's a sad commentary that numerous books have appeared over the last several years centered around the theme of "nature-deficit disorder" in our children.[48] Nature is a rich resource for connecting us to the earth, soothing the soul, and inspiring creativity. Tragically, many of today's children are missing out on the opportunity to have this kind of experience. As we discussed in earlier, outings to state or national parks and nature preserves provide memorable family fieldtrips. However, sometimes such trips are difficult for families to make, either because of time, distance, or economic factors.

If you can't get to a large, protected natural space, don't despair. Your own backyard can be a treasure for nature exploration. As you read ahead, please keep in mind that if you don't have an outside garden, raising plants indoors can be a very nurturing experience for your child as well.

In your yard, there may be grass, with or without dandelions, three- and four-leafed clovers, flowering plants and bushes, trees, and more. And with those things usually come a variety of insects, birds, and critters like squirrels and chipmunks. Even these seemingly common aspects of nature bring out the inherent curiosity in children. They notice rocks, flowers, feathers, leaves, earthworms, spiderwebs, and even morning dew.

As we discussed at length in the last chapter, if you live in an environment where it's possible, you might consider gardening—even container gardening to start with, which works well if you live in an urban area with limited space. Children love planting seeds and watching them grow; they especially love harvesting vegetables, herbs, or fruits that they have planted or helped to plant and tend. You can also set up birdbaths, birdfeeders (including hummingbird feeders), and squirrel feeders. Children can watch the different kinds of wildlife that show up to eat, drink, and bathe. They can learn the names of different kinds of birds, flowers, trees, and more, and they can begin to understand the importance of biodiversity, even in smaller spaces.

Children also enjoy making things out of objects and materials found in nature—stick boats, hollyhock dolls, bouquets from flowers, a bow and arrow out of maple twigs. They build rock structures, construct faerie houses from pieces of bark, make swords from sticks, and create collages from flowers and pinecones. Put them in nature, and children will readily find—or create—things to do.

You don't have to be a nature aficionado or even particularly like the outdoors to expose your children to it once in a while. There are many ways to have a family nature adventure—from going on a picnic in a park, to taking a naturalist-led day hike at a local nature preserve, to camping as a family.

> *The Murillo kids can't wait for their annual three-day family beach trip with all of their cousins. Why? Because each year they plan to make a bigger, better, and more elaborate sand-castle than the one they made the year before. As the trip gets closer, they start talking about the castle's design, including the moats, turrets, and perimeter areas. When the day finally*

arrives, they are up early and ready to go. They work together to decide on the location and size of the sandcastle, and they divide up the necessary tasks and figure out who's taking care of the water features, who's doing the digging, and who's on turret detail. They don't always agree; in fact, they disagree quite a bit. However, they work together and compromise. They are also pretty good at taking turns. They work for hours on end, occasionally asking a parent to do some digging or heavy lifting. The end result doesn't always look like their plan, but each creation is interesting and satisfying. And, more importantly, the children get to spend time immersed in nature in a place they like with people they love engaged in a continually unfolding creative collaboration.

Even if you live in the middle of a big city, nature usually isn't that far away. Most areas have public parks of some kind. Sometimes museums have sculpture gardens outside of them that look enough like parks to qualify as a decent outdoor space. Be open to anything green!

A book we recommend for budding creativity in nature (pun intended), especially for those who have a penchant for design and invention, is *Biomimicry: Inventions Inspired by Nature* by Dora Lee (2011). This book is rich with visuals and stories. Sections include Learning from Mother Nature; Nature Thought of It First; Smart Structures; Computing, Nature's Way; and Nature's Nanotechnology. A sample story that directly connects nature with the creative process is the story of Swiss inventor George de Mestral, who noticed how stubbornly burrs stuck to his pants. Curious, he examined one under a microscope, and he found that the burr's hook-like shape gave it the perfect form to cling to the mini-looped structure of the fabric of his pants. This careful observation led him to the development of Velcro! Stories like this one get children thinking about what they might be able to do with the right ideas and inspiration.

Being in nature for a child is like being in a large art studio and a hands-on science lab combined. Many describe the experience using statements like "All of my problems seem to go away," or "My mind becomes clear and calm." As the famous naturalist John Muir once said, "The power of imagination makes us infinite." We can only imagine that this thought came to him while he was exploring the wilderness.

Local Fieldtrips

One day, when Susan was living in Chicago, as she walked down one of the main streets in the downtown area she saw a crowd at the corner looking up, pointing, and talking excitedly. The group was speaking in a foreign language, and many of them had cameras with them. It was a group of visitors from another country, and they were pointing to a clock that protruded from the corner of a century-old department store—a clock that Susan had seen countless times before.

The episode piqued Susan's interest. After a bit of research, she discovered that the Marshall Field's department store was—at that time—the second largest store in the world, that it had survived the Great Chicago Fire, and that the blue-patina clock at the corner of it, circa 1897, weighed 7.5 tons. Now that's interesting!

So what does this story tell us? Well, sometimes when we live in a place for a while, we take for granted the many interesting things that are in that place. Many environments—urban, small-town, and rural—have treasures right under our noses. And exploring our close-to-home environment can be a great source of inspiration.

We are strong proponents of family fieldtrips. We think of these as enrichment experiences—a bit like the family adventures that we've discussed, but they can be closer to home.

Janine Walker Caffrey, author of *Nurturing Brilliance: Discovering and Developing Your Child's Gifts* (2011), supports this concept too, and she organizes her recommendations around children's particular areas of interest or ability. For instance, children with a precocity for words often like bookstores, libraries, puppet shows, and plays. Kids who have strong math interests might want to explore chess clubs, buildings with interesting architecture, or invention museums. The zoo, of course, is always a great spot for young scientists to sit, observe, sketch, and write field notes. These kids also like technology stores or any place containing gadgets. Youngsters with strong interpersonal leadership abilities and a deep concern for others might enjoy spending a day with a local chapter of Habitat for Humanity or at a Red Cross food drive. Budding artists and designers will appreciate art museums, architecture walks, botanical gardens, and art workshops. Young musicians will want to explore a variety of concerts, music stores, and street fairs. Dancers will be eager to attend dance concerts and recitals. They also may enjoy ice skating, rollerblading, surfing, or any other activity in which they can immerse their whole bodies. Athletes love attending sports events or finding great outdoor play spaces; they also like tobogganing, white water rafting, and other adventure trips. And this is just a start of what might work for a family fieldtrip.

The National Park Service provides "passports" to people who want to explore America's national parks. When you take the passport with you, you can get a special stamp from each park you visit. On a recent trip to Washington, DC, Susan's family discovered that Ford's Theatre, where President Lincoln was shot, is considered a national historic site in the national park system; it is, technically, a national park. What a great way to spend a few hours feeding the imagination by immersing yourself in the past! There are nearly 400 sites within the national park system, so the National Park Service's website (www.nps.gov/index.htm) is yet another resource for finding unique places near you.

Many cities have youth guides that have less conventional recommendations for outings. Susan, who formerly lived primarily in Southern California, now spends more of her time at home in the San Francisco Bay Area and she loves exploring using creative guides like *Frommer's San Francisco with Kids* and *City Walks with Kids.* Here's one example from the Frommer guide: "Walk #25—Eagle's Point: Imagine you're Peter Pan or Wendy as you forsake civilization to trek through misty forests, gaze out over rugged cliffs, and reach a hidden cove." When parents take their children on such outings, they not only get to experience the adventures for themselves, they also get the added benefit of seeing things from a child's perspective of fresh excitement and wonder.

Boosting Creative Potential—Creative Environments, At Home and Away

As you can see, your child's creative environment does not have boundaries. Creative experiences can be approached flexibly, extending beyond the walls of your dwelling into your garage, yard, city, and vacation spot. A child's world is her playground, and you get to decide how big or small that playground is, as well what it contains. Remember that a creative environment includes creating a family atmosphere of exploration, taking creative risks, and respecting everyone's ideas. It involves allowing your child time by herself, time with you, and time for adventure. Whether in your home, in your town, or in the great outdoors, you are the role model—the creative mentor, if you will—who can shape, influence, and demonstrate openness to discovery and imagination for your child. We encourage you to relish the adventure.

Chapter 8
Creative Projects and Technology—A World of Possibilities in the Palm of Your Hand

Note: Content for this chapter was contributed by two of Susan's graduate students—elementary teacher, Donna Drake, and film and video instructor, JT Chaiyakam.

We all carry the power of creative technology in our hands every day. Phones are ubiquitous, iPads too. Young children know how to swipe to get to a game or app they want. They are adept consumers of technology. Slightly older children actively create video moments and snap photos of their pets, foods, and friends and their stories with social media.

The cellphone's magic can create digital paintings, snap stunning photographs, compose music, solve math problems, design video games, edit essays, and even create movies. And there are thousands of tutorials online to help you at every step of the process.

Certainly, some technological tools that are available today may vanish tomorrow. But technology will continue to grow and innovate. Like a pencil and a sheet of paper, technology is a creative tool. Not to disparage the pencil, but an innovative program like photoshop has a few more bells and whistles. And thanks to the cellphone (or augmented reality contact lenses, if you are reading this in 2025), we can use technology to boost our children's creativity. And for students who may be struggling to find their voice, it might be the best option for them to express themselves when the paper and pencil fails to provide the means to do so—especially so for students who are strong visual thinkers.

As parents, teachers, and advocates, we can use these tools to discover novel ways for our children to play and communicate new ideas. Children can improve understanding and retain information through novel and authentic methods. For some students, their only creative path may be with technological tools.

Using Technology for Creative Production

Many people think of the internet as the information highway. If that is so, then technology has provided creative thinkers a great new path for product generation. Some fields in the technology world are experiences in and of themselves, but many of your child's everyday mini c and little c activities can be enriched through the use of technology.

Creativity is often related to thinking of new or different ways of doing things or it can also be expanding on something we already do. Technology is simply a tool that helps us achieve these aspects that come naturally to creative thinkers. It allows us to move beyond our traditional thinking as we find ways to weave technology into projects a child may already be exploring. So we are going to think of this section of the book as being an idea generator for ways to incorporate technology into creativity.

To begin, we should address two items of importance. It is important not to limit your thinking. Sometimes the areas your child selects for creativity may surprise you and adding technology may not be any different. There are some children who prefer the hands-on feeling of building with Legos and may hate virtual building apps and games. But there are some children who show no interest building with Legos, yet excel at the three dimensional building games such as Minecraft and Terraria. Or they may fluctuate between the virtual world and the hands-on aspects of creating. Remember that for many creative people it is the process of creating and not the finished product that can motivate them. Technology allows us to explore new avenues in our world of creating, but it should not pigeonhole us into one aspect of creative thinking.

Another important aspect of technology is the one of online safety. As a parent, it is your job to set parameters and ensure the safety of your child if they embark in online endeavors. Many children want an authentic audience, but do not have the maturity to filter out important personal information such as their age, the name of the town where they live (or famous landmarks), or school they attend. If your child wants to create a vlog, look for ones that feature parent controls and are designed for kids. Or find a way to share it yourself, such as emailing it to close relatives that you trust. Some parents have concerns about the amount of time children spend using technology and while it is a great asset, we also recognize and encourage the benefits of outdoor time and hands on experiences. Digital citizenship is critical in today's technological world and you and your child need to find a level of use that brings a measure of comfort and safety as well as creative expression.

Now on to idea generation! These are ideas to get you started. Many of these can become interdisciplinary involving language skills, math, science, art and more. Take them and run with them!

- The at home chef may move from experimenting in their kitchen to providing tutorials for others online or creating a vlog of their favorite menu items. They may become restaurant critics, record reviews of their meals, and cite their preference for one restaurant's French fries over another's. They could expand this to taking polls and surveys and offer ratings and rankings. Perhaps they want to experiment with one food and decide which method of cooking or ingredient provides the best results and then play with the presentation of their entree or dessert. Perhaps they want to design their own restaurant and create commercials (digital print or video) for it.

- For those children who excel at organization, they may record their collections (stamps, dolls, sands from around the world) in a database and eventually create a picture catalogue. This could be for their own use, or it could be used to inform relatives of "missing elements" needed for the collection. It could be turned into a brochure or booklet informing others on the topic. Or perhaps they want to create an infographic on how to start and organize collections.
- The child who loves creating puppet shops may discover that stop-motion movie making is a desirable medium for their storytelling. They child who has adventures in cardboard creating small castles and forts may now use them as backdrops for small film productions - after they have researched medieval construction on the internet first. As a group project, you may experience the synergy of one person creating the set, another the script, one the costumes, and another doing publicity and advertising.
- Small businesses have been started when adventurous parents purchase 3D printers and let their children take over. These printers allow children to implement their own engineering and spatial designs and make adaptations and improvements to them. Under certain conditions, they may develop a plan for marketing, publicity, and consumer relations. Or perhaps your child is building a model railroad and wants to design the buildings and landscape to place around the tracks. A

future anthropologist may make models of different skeletal structures. There are many products designed for kids and many adults who are enjoying them as well!

- Game design is also a high interest activity, especially for teens. If they are not playing a game, they are creating videos of their latest conquests, providing tutorials on how to advance game playing skills, and some have even moved into the world of coding and create their own programs. Budding engineers and architects may find different aesthetics to add to their virtual designs and venture into Computer Aided Design.
- Avid readers often balk at having to write a formal book review. But what if they could portray a character and record the story from the character's perspective. For a stirring (and professionally done) video book retelling watch the video Wishtree by Katherin Applegate on YouTube and it will surely inspire young filmmakers after they have read a book. Ask a local bookstore if they would be willing to put your child's creation on their website.
- Entire bands and concerts have been created from electronically generated instruments. This is a fun way for the up-and-coming composer to experiment with a new instrument, style, or genre that may intrigue them. Sound editing can be a great addition to those gaming videos, theater productions, or the next blockbuster action-adventure movie. Sound bites can be a great addition when your young animal researcher wants to explain the different calls of a loon or the variations of a jazz improvisation.
- Technology also allows us to streamline projects, generate possibilities and make selections.
- Software allows us to "try on" different glasses and make the perfect selection. Your young fashion designer or theater costumer will expand on this idea generating various styles in many color options without having to cut a single piece of fabric. Quilt designers can play with block arrangements

and layouts digitally rather than scattering pieces across a bed or pinned to the carpet.

- Photographers can edit photos, experiment with various filters, and create digital or mixed media scrapbooks to document family trips and local adventures. Videos can often be incorporated into these as well, so you have a mixture of live action with still shots. They can then weave stories throughout the photos, and you have the makings of family folklore, or perhaps the truth behind the lore!
- Genealogists used to have lengthy scrolls with names taped and written on them to map lineage (at least that was our initial experience) that you hid under the bed between use. But now you can format them into various charts and diagrams that can be artfully displayed and shared with others. These artifacts can then be used as a springboard into interviewing activities, a topic that is discussed in more detail in the next chapter.

Hopefully these ideas have sparked your own thinking because there are certainly many more ideas out there! Keep in mind that technology is an additional tool in your child's pocket that they can choose to use in enhancing their creativity. As with any tool, it may take time and practice to become proficient and your child may choose to abandon it for a time. Exploring technology can add to the creative process and product, but it is not a requirement. As you listen to your child, you will discover the ways you can best support them when it comes to incorporating technology with creativity. Most importantly, remember to have fun!

Making Movies

JT has introduced students to the use of boom microphones, lighting gear, higher-end cameras, sound recorders, green screens, and an endless number of cables to connect all his gadgets while shooting short films in his classroom. When the 2020 pandemic forced students and teachers online, he had to rethink how to shoot movies with the students. He quickly realized these movies do not require all the expensive gadgets. The cellphone is all you need to create great stories.

The best place to start is with what you both already know: Home and family. Your creative child can interview you, their siblings, and other family members. They can ask questions or give answers about their family pet, or create a funny story about their grandparents. We each have so many tales and hidden dreams ready to be documented. Think of this creative exercise as a photo album transformed into a short movie. Children readily find the video camera the perfect way to tell a story.

In one of JT's film workshops, Aiden, a quiet ten-year-old, wanted to create a video about his dog, Bailey. JT shared with Aiden and his mother step-by-step instructions on how to go from script to screen. The process is described below. This video story is about how Aiden and Bailey met. But you could apply these steps to any interview-style storytelling. So, while we walk through Aiden and Bailey's story, think about how you might use this video design process and some of the tools to create a video story with your child.

Brainstorming

Now that we picked our subject, Bailey, what do you want to say about Bailey? How did Bailey become part of the family? Can Bailey do any tricks? What makes Bailey special? What's the funniest story about Bailey? Why did you name him Bailey? What else should we ask about Bailey?

Bailey is a 4-year-old Golden Retriever who had three owners before he came to live with Aiden. The first time Aiden saw Bailey, he wanted him to be his dog. Unfortunately, Bailey was the neighbor's pet, but that didn't prevent Aiden from visiting Bailey almost every day. A year later, the neighbors were moving to Florida and couldn't take Bailey with them. So Aiden was able to have his own dog.

Interviews

Now Aiden gets to choose who tells all the stories about Bailey. Will he choose his mother, who said yes to having Bailey? Will he choose his little sister, Grace, who loves Bailey just as much? Or maybe

Aiden will tell the story himself. Aiden chose to interview his family about Bailey, and he decided that he would be the main narrator connecting the story elements of Bailey's joining the family.

Lights, Camera, Action

The term "lights" is used loosely. A well-lit room or natural sunlight is perfect for shooting videos. Be sure to have your light source facing your subject. Facing an open window gives perfect day lighting. Generally, interview set-ups are a single camera on a medium close-up shot of your subject—about 2 inches above the subject's head to about the middle of their chest. However, you can bend the rules and create closer video shots or farther shots if the location is relevant.

Camera tripods are fine if you want steady video shots. But it's only an option. There are plenty of professional documentarians who like free-flowing camera movements. But it's essential to always keep your subject in the camera frame.

Filming

Back in the brainstorming and interview stage, Aiden already developed a blueprint on what to film. First, he begins with a visual introduction of himself with narration. Next, he will focus on interviews with his family. And of course, there will be lots of videos of the film's star - Bailey - doing tricks and enjoying his family. It's helpful to organize these in three parts: (1) Aiden's introduction, (2) the interviews, and (3) lots of footage of Bailey. Aiden will film everything on the camera to secure his footage, He can transfer to the editing app later. That way, he will have all of the videos secure on his camera and separate from the editing app.

Editing

Once Aiden compiled the multiple film segments, the process became a bit like a puzzle. First, it's time to sort all of the pieces and then design how to put the pieces together. For Bailey's story, Aiden used FilmoraGo, one of the most user-friendly apps available for iOS and Android phones. Most parents and children seem to learn the basics in an hour.

Next steps include: trim (edit) the chosen video clips, then - add music, sound effects, filters, and transitions between clips. If the video needs more narration, many apps have a microphone feature that allows you to narrate your video directly. Luckily the apps have their own tutorials, and you can find dozens of useful tutorials on YouTube. Many of these apps are intuitive, and if you play with all the features, you and your creative child will find novel ways to tell your story.

The Story of Bailey

Aiden's short story has an introduction, videos of his dog—Bailey, interviews with his family telling short stories about Bailey, and a conclusion from Aiden on why he loves his dog so much. He added music, filters, and fun transitions between video clips. It was a project that involved the whole family.

Aiden was able to express himself through the Four P's of Creativity—Person, Process, Products, and Press/Environment. He was able to think creatively and make choices through his mother's guidance. Aiden chose the subject, brainstormed the questions, and looked for answers like a detective. He had an environment welcoming to his creativity and a final project he shared with his teachers, friends, and family.

The steps and structure of video albums can fit many different stories. No matter what you are filming, the same steps from brainstorming to editing are recommended. Brainstorming is the time to be creatively wild, but once you and your creative child have settled on a story, you can follow the organizational steps laid out for Aiden and his dog Bailey.

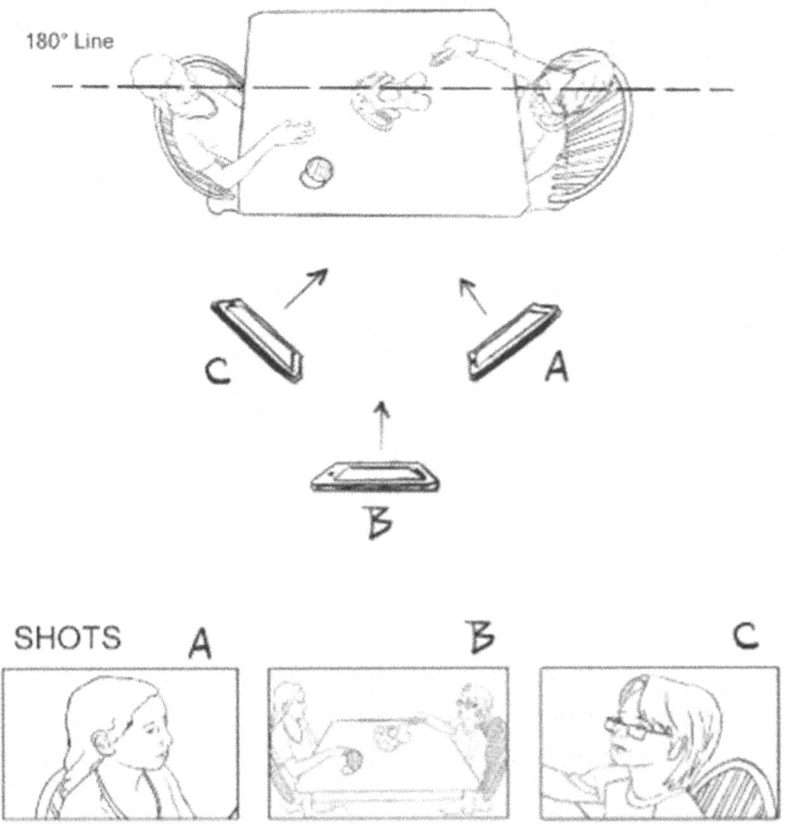

Grace and Anna

In another example, Grace, 10, wants to create a film about her 5-year-old baby sister, Anna. Since Grace doesn't have many videos of her sister as a baby, she can use old photos and videos to tell a story.

Grace has decided to narrate the entire video about how she first felt being a big sister and how she currently feels about a big sister's role.

Although Grace knew clearly about what pictures she wanted to use, she was unsure about the narration and videos. Grace and her parents worked together and discussed what they would like to make with Anna. They decided videos of them playing together would work for this visual story. Much like Aiden and his dog, Grace and Anna should be evenly framed. This camera angle is called a two-shot (because it contains two subjects). While a two-shot is great for basic images, Grace wanted it to look more like a movie. Over the shoulder shots afforded different angles of Grace and Anna playing. And inserts captured special closeups like playing with toys, and closeups of Anna laughing and playing. The additional video footage gives their video album dynamic variety. Once all the videos were shot and approved, they started editing in their phone editing app. The following illustration provides you with a variety of additional shots. The dotted line is 180 degrees, creating a specific orientation of the subjects to the camera. In making movies, it's best to stay on one side of the 180-degree line to create a continuity of multiple shots. Crossing the line may make it appear Grace and Anna are not looking at each other in closer shots. It's a rule that filmmakers try not to break in movies big and small.

Now that Grace had a two-minute edited video, she felt comfortable recording narration. Together they worked on a script and recorded directly in the phone app. In Grace's narration, she described not wanting a baby sister at first. Now that she has Anna in her life, Grace loves her very much and wants to be a great big sister and a best friend. With some music, this became a fantastic video these sisters can cherish for a lifetime. These videos are more than just a creative activity. They become pieces of art that connect families and promote social and emotional bonding.

Grandpa's Stories

Jake, 10, is another student that didn't care much about brainstorming and writing, but he still loved retelling personal and family stories. He loved his grandfather's stories about being a pilot in the military. Making a video was a perfect opportunity to preserve his grandfather's story and give Jake a new creative outlet. For the interview, Jake asked his grandfather the following three questions to make the video short and concise:

- Why did you want to be a fighter pilot?
- What is the scariest part about flying?
- What is your favorite part about flying?

Together, Jake and his grandfather sat together and created a five-minute video together. In this video album, the sit-down interview became the narration. In editing, Jake added pictures and videos to cut away from the interview. In editing, sometimes it is necessary to separate the audio from the video image. If you plan to add photos and videos, separating the audio allows you to cut and move audio clips to match your images. Because of Jake's relationship with his grandfather much of the brainstorming and planning came quickly and naturally. Jake's interview with his grandfather could be a one-time short interview, or if he shows continued interests, Jake could create a series of interviews.

All of the student video producers we've discussed - Jake, Grace, and Aiden—could continue making short videos as long as they continue to be inspired to create. There are countless family stories, vacations, siblings, and relatives to tell about and interview. If your creative child loves to share ideas, information, and opinions, filming videos might be a perfect creative medium.

As Far as Your Imagination Can Take You

Although we have discussed family events to teach students and parents movie making, there is always the creative child who loves telling imaginative stories. For those of you who have such a child, embrace it and have fun. There is no need to add extra structure or pressure of writing scripts and storyboarding the movie. Like my examples, children can brainstorm an idea, create an outline of what they want to make with what they already have in the house. I've seen ghost stories, detective stories, and superhero stories created with a child's imagination and beautifully depicted in short movies. We live in an amazing time. You have an entire production studio built into your phone. Play and have fun!

JTs Recommendations for Video Apps

> **FilmoraGo** is recommended for editing movies directly on the phone. It is intuitive and gives flexibility without being overly complicated. There are dozens of editing apps available for iOS and Android. These apps all have various functions—from managing music to creating filters and fun transitions between clips. Most importantly, students can easily download and start shooting videos and edit them into beautiful short stories.

The power of storytelling is limitless. Beyond filming, there are many creative apps available on the phone. What if your creative child wants to create animation or draw?

> **Flipaclip** - Flipaclip is a cartoon animation app that many artistic children pick up right away. Students can add backgrounds, music, audio tracks, and narrate animated clips. One student enjoyed drawing comic strips for his classmates. He would make dozens of copies and hand them out. With Flipaclip, he transformed his comics into a lively animated short clip and shared them with the entire school. You can use your fingers to draw directly on your phone, although some children may be more accustomed to a pencil. Stylus pens are relatively inexpensive to purchase.

> **Stop Motion Studio** - If your creative child is interested in making toys, cutout art, or Legos come alive, this might be the perfect app. You can take multiple still pictures directly in the app and instantly animate any toy or Legos. It has many functions, from simple snap and moving your objects to green screen opportunities

if your child wants to explore more complex creations. Some fantastic artists are experimenting with Stop Motion Studio. This app is suggested for children that want to combine physical art with video art. There are additional costs, but they are minimal.

Procreate Pocket - This is a bonus app for your creative child. Think about the illustrations in these chapters. In one image, you can tell a whole story. Procreate can be used on a tablet and also has a pocket (mobile) version for both iOS and Android. Procreate Pocket is excellent for new artists but can also meet the needs of more advanced creators. You can draw and paint with hundreds of brush strokes. It is a perfect doodling app for children that need a little artistic recreation. Much like Flipaclip, some creative children may prefer a stylus pen.

Boosting Creativity with Technology

Technology and screens are an everyday part of kids' lives, and while we need to be mindful about the amount and type of technology used, there are many ways technology can enhance and contribute to the creative process for children and teens.

Technology allows for moving beyond the typical ways of creating by offering several modalities to stretch one's knowledge, research, collections, music, storytelling, cooking, filming, and virtually all forms of art. When it comes to boosting your child's creativity, technology offers many applications that will allow your child to explore their creative potential, engage in a creative process, and provide multiple possible pathways to a creative product.

Chapter 9
Parenting Creative Children and Teens

So far you have learned about types of creativity, components of the creative process, creative personality traits, and strategies for cultivating creativity in your children. At this point, you are probably asking, "So how do I parent my wonderfully (though often exhausting) creative child?" Our ideas about parenting creative children come from four primary sources: two significant books, our experiences working with creative children and their parents, and raising our own creative kids.

The first book was written by two researchers with the Boston College School of Education in the early 1990s. John Dacey, Ph.D., and Alex Packer, Ph.D., were interested in the causes—or at least the influencing factors—of creativity in young people. They compiled a team of psychologists and educators to select participants from a group of creative students who were nominated by teachers, counselors, and program directors at schools for the gifted in New England. The nominations were based solely on creative accomplishments and not on test scores, grades, or any other type of school performance. In the end, 56 families and 100 children participated in the study. A description of this study, along with sage advice and many examples, is presented and explained in the book *The Nurturing Parent: How to Raise Creative, Loving, Responsible Children* (Dacey and Packer, 1992).

As you may have guessed from their book's title, Dacey and Packer discovered a particular type of parenting style which they call the "Nurturing Parent." Some people who hear that term today think of what we now call "helicopter parents"—over-involved and over-indulgent moms and dads who swoop in to solve problems that kids should solve themselves, which deprives the children of opportunities to grow into resilient, independent adults. This concern has been discussed in books like Bronson and Merryman's *Nurture Shock*,[67] as well as a plethora of articles and essays on the topic. Indeed, Dacey and Packer themselves comment on the rising concerns of overindulgence and over-nurturing in today's parenting styles. However, they assert that the Nurturing Parent style does *not* result in overindulgence or over-protection, but instead speaks to a parenting approach of both nurturing and support, which are key elements in raising independent, responsible, and empathic children.

Before discussing the Nurturing Parent style in depth, we want to provide a brief overview of three other common parenting styles. They are: (1) authoritarian parenting, (2) permissive parenting, and (3) authoritative parenting.

Authoritarian parenting is considered a form of "old school" or traditional parenting. It is based largely on parental controls and rules that are strictly enforced. Children who are raised in this parenting style may achieve well enough, but they often are overly concerned with pleasing others and with what others think rather than with achieving goals and successes for their own inner satisfaction. They are typically good at playing by the rules and doing the "right" things, and they may try to stay under the radar so as not to get in trouble. Children raised with this approach often find it difficult to step "out of the box" and follow their own path.

The *permissive parenting style* is the opposite of authoritarian parenting; the parents don't discipline much, and they exert little or no control over their children. Children with permissive parents are at risk for having low self-control and little or no sense of responsibility, since they aren't expected to demonstrate either.

They are often anxious or rebellious, because they don't know what their boundaries and limits are. Rather than growing up with a sense of freedom from their permissive parents, these children actually may be fearful and might even feel a lack of safety or security due to the lack of boundaries that have been set for them.

Authoritative parenting tends to be the most modern, most popular parenting style at present. Authoritative parents work toward a careful balance of being authoritarian when needed yet permissive at other times. These parents tend to back off when things are going well and get more involved with limits when things aren't going so well. In this model, children sometimes are allowed input into decisions, but parents typically have the final say. Children raised in this parenting model generally become independent and cooperative adults, yet they often look to others for validation and as a result may not have a strong sense of who they are as unique individuals.

The Nurturing Parent

The parenting style that supports the development of creative, responsible, and thoughtful youth is that of the Nurturing Parent. Dacey and Packer found that this parenting style involves respecting children's thoughts and feelings and encouraging them to determine their own priorities rather than having others decide for them. These parents have clear values and actively encourage self-discipline, commitment, and intellectual and creative freedom in their children. Central to this parenting style is that the parents make it a priority to let their children learn from experience rather than through imposed consequences. They believe that children need practice making their own choices and decisions in order to learn how to use good judgment and ultimately become responsible adults.

Specifically, Dacey and Packer found that parents of creative children exhibit the following six behaviors:

- They *trust* their child's fairness and good judgment.
- They *respect* their child's autonomy, thoughts, and feelings.
- They *support* their child's interests and goals.
- They *enjoy* their child's company.
- They *protect* their child from hurting him- or herself or others.
- They *model* self-control, sensitivity, and values they believe are important.

Let's look at each of these qualities of the Nurturing Parent and consider how they support independence, responsibility, and creativity in children.

Trust

Nurturing parents trust that their child is going to make good decisions because they themselves model good decisions and promote high moral standards. This type of parenting involves *listening* to your child rather than *reacting* to what she says, allowing her to have her own thoughts and ideas instead of trying to impose yours onto her, and trying not to fix problems that crop up for her. A key factor in being able to do this is promoting communication by being nonjudgmental of your child's behaviors or the situations in which she finds herself.

Let's have a look at some examples that illustrate the role that trust plays in developing creative thinking abilities in children. Rachel asks her mother, "What should I do? My friend Mattie said she doesn't want to be my friend anymore. She ate lunch with someone else today and wouldn't even save a seat for me. I'm so mad at her!" Rachel's mother listens intently but does not try to fix the problem. Instead, she says to Rachel, "I can see that you're upset. What ideas do you have for how to deal with this?"

Luis can't decide whether or not to tell his teacher that another student is cheating off of him on tests. He talks to his father about it, saying, "I don't want to get anyone in trouble, but I don't feel it's right for him to copy my work, either. I don't know what to do." Luis's father validates that his son is in a difficult situation and asks him, "Well, what do you think your options are?" Luis then must brainstorm the various steps that he could take to address the situation. He discusses these aloud with his dad. At the end of the conversation, his father asks him if he knows what he is going to do.

In situations like these, Rachel's mother and Luis's father clearly show that they trust their child's ability to make good decisions and to deal with the consequences of their actions. If these parents were to tell their children what to do, they would be undermining the children's opportunity to make an important decision and to have confidence in themselves to make future decisions.

Respect

As you may have noticed, your creative child has a mind and a style all his own. Nurturing Parents show respect for their child's individuality and decisions, even the bad ones! Admittedly, that's not easy. But you have to consider what behaviors you are reinforcing. Is it more important for your child to make the "right" decision (the decision that you want him to make), or is it better to encourage him to stand behind his own decisions and deal with the consequences of them? Can you separate yourself from your child's decisions and let him own those choices?

Molly is a competitive gymnast—and a very good one at that. But the training and competing come with a price: Molly spends nearly all of her time outside of school working on her gymnastics. After years of not being able to participate in "regular" teen activities, Molly decides that it's time to take a break from competing to spend more time with her friends. Her mother, who has spent an equal amount of time (and a great deal of money) with her daughter waiting at practices, working with coaches, and traveling across the country to competitions, is suddenly faced with a very difficult decision: Does she push her child toward the future she believes is best, or does she support Molly's significant life decision? Could you respect Molly's newly chosen path? It sounds pretty tough, doesn't it? We know! But consider the alternative, and see if you can understand why forcing Molly to continue to do what she doesn't want to do will demonstrate to her a distinct lack of respect for her opinions and feelings, not to mention her ability to choose her own course in life.

Support

Certainly it's a good thing when parents show interest in their children's goals and passions and actively support them. But support does not mean excessive praise. As Teresa Amabile and others in the creativity field have noted, excessive praise or false praise is a "creativity killer."[68] Excessive praise turns kids into praise junkies, and they start to do things just for praise rather than for inner satisfaction. However, moderate praise for effort is appropriate; as parents, we want to encourage persistence and hard work.

Rewards are another concept not to be confused with support. Rewarding children for their work makes them less motivated and less creative, and it makes their work less enjoyable to them.[69] It is important for parents to minimize the use of rewards and praise and to encourage children to reward themselves. Instead of saying, "You're the best!" "You're really talented!" or "You're a natural!" (all comments that focus on innate ability rather than on the effort it takes to do well at something), ask your child about specific elements of her accomplishment—for example, "What do you like about your drawing? What do you think is the best part? Is there anything you want to change?" This kind of question gets children reflecting on their work and giving themselves feedback.

We want children to remain intrinsically (internally) motivated by their interests and passions rather than extrinsically (externally) motivated. The latter often results in the "What do I get if I do it?" question, which suggests that the motivation no longer comes from within. Recall the Goldilocks Principle: You don't want to give out too much or too little praise, but instead just the right amount of positive feedback.

Enjoyment

This may sound surprisingly obvious in its simplicity, but Dacey and Packer found that Nurturing Parents enjoy their kids. They spend time together working on projects, talking, planning, and traveling. They value their children's opinions and truly consider them. They are interested in their children's projects, ideas, and goals and welcome the opportunity to discuss them. However, please don't start thinking that you are a bad parent because you need an occasional break from your child. And don't fret over your last argument with him, worrying that it proves you don't enjoy him. You can enjoy your child, appreciate him, and value him while still acknowledging the challenges of parenting.

Protection

Interestingly, Dacey and Packer found that nurturing families have fewer rules than most other families have. This lack of rules does not mean permissive parenting or a lack of limits. Instead, Nurturing Parents set their limits through communication and discussion. There are definite expectations for behavior, and there are clearly defined limits. If there is a problem, the parents discuss with the child her behavior, as well as the impact her behavior has on others. When there is a major disagreement about limits, Nurturing Parents often will try a compromise first rather than an iron-fist approach. Trust, respect, discussion, compromise—these, and not rules, are the ingredients that Nurturing Parents use to protect their children from harm.

Sometimes, though, limits and boundaries have to be upheld in uncompromising fashion. There are times when a child wants to do things that could have dramatic and damaging effects on her life or her future. For example, if a child wants to attend a concert with friends in another city before she is ready, or go to a party without adults present, or get a tattoo or piercing that she may later regret, a Nurturing Parent doesn't hesitate to set firm limits to protect her from potentially harmful situations. When safety is a concern, Nurturing Parents step in and establish clear boundaries for their children.

Role Modeling

Nurturing Parents model the values and responsibilities that they hope their children will develop. It is the way they live, rather than the rules they set, that maintains discipline in the home. Dacey and Packer state: "Children are more likely to do what you do, not what you say. The parents in our study don't preach to their children about the values of hard work; they work hard. They don't lecture on the importance of honesty and tolerance; they try to lead honest and tolerant lives."[70]

This is all good news! You don't have to be more creative than your child, and you don't have to be a child psychologist to analyze your child's psyche. Role modeling means that by living the type of life you think is important and engaging in the activities that are important to you, you are teaching your child desirable values and behaviors. A critical point to be aware of is that creative children tend to notice inconsistencies and inauthentic behavior in others, so it is much easier to teach your child with a "do as I do" approach than a "do as I say" one.

More Suggestions

Through their extensive interviews of parents of creative youth, Dacey and Packer found that the Nurturing Parent approach is responsible for raising not only creative, but also responsible, empathic, and hard-working kids. They had set out to look for components of creativity and discovered that the parents of the creative children all exhibited the same fundamental parenting characteristics.

But we were left scratching our heads, because our experience with creative children is that while many of them are hard-working, many others exhibit challenges with task completion, have trouble performing consistently in school, and are not stellar at carrying out basic tasks at home. Then it hit us. The children in Dacey and Packer's study had been nominated based on "creative accomplishment." These were kids who had succeeded in bringing to completion a creative project that was seen as valuable by educators—things like winning an innovative math award, writing and producing a play, having artwork selected for a local museum exhibit, and so on. So it seems that the Nurturing Parent approach contributes to raising creative *and* productive children. You might be thinking, "That sounds great, but my child is not quite there yet. Help!"

At the beginning of this chapter, we told you that our suggestions and recommendations for parenting creative children come in part from two books. The first is the one we just discussed by Dacey and Packer. The second book is Dr. Lucy Jo Palladino's *Dreamers, Discoverers, and Dynamos: How to Help the Child Who Is Bright, Bored, and Having Problems in School* (formerly titled *The Edison Trait,* 1999). Drawing on decades of clinical practice as a psychologist, Dr. Lucy Jo Palladino describes three different types of creative children. First are the Dreamers, who have strong imaginations and live in their own imaginary worlds. Second are the Discoverers, who spend their time investigating, exploring, and doing things their own way. Third are the Dynamos, who have high energy levels, love to take risks, and thrive on personal challenge.

The book was originally titled *The Edison Trait* because Dr. Palladino found that creative children often do not conform, do not fit, are divergent thinkers, and exhibit many other characteristics frequently attributed to the great inventor Thomas Edison, who is known to have daydreamed so much in his brief three months of formal schooling that his teacher called him "addled." Thereafter, Edison's mother taught him at home, where he was free to display all of the quirky characteristics so common among gifted and creative children. These include a daring or wondering imagination, creative urges or a compelling attraction to new ideas, a global perspective, and an intense focus on and persistence in areas of passion and interest.

Palladino also describes the sometimes-troublesome characteristics of Edison-trait children from the perspective of many parents and teachers. These include being easily distracted and disorganized, neglecting important details, leaving projects and activities incomplete, and being resistant to direction.

Now you might be saying, "Yep. Right. That's my child. So what can I as a parent do to help him be successful?" You might also say, "My child is everything on that list, and he is totally exhausting!"

We know that these kids can be exhausting. We also know from the work of Dacey and Packer and Palladino, and our own experiences as well, that these young people have the capacity to be caring and responsible while also maintaining a fair amount of independence and creative expression. The question then becomes, "How can I help my creative child have that too?" You are among many parents searching for the answer, and we have some recommendations that will help. Here we go.

Understand Your Mindset

A mindset—the way we think about ourselves and others—is a central element of parenting style and how we think about our children. Carol Dweck's work on this topic is widely accepted as an important parenting and teaching paradigm. In short, Dweck (2008) writes about *fixed* versus *growth* mindsets. Let us explain.

People with a fixed mindset believe that they are born with all the abilities they will ever have, whereas those with the growth mindset believe that they are evolving, complex human beings who can and will improve with hard work and practice. This concept is key to our current discussion for two reasons. First, you need to be aware of your own mindset when parenting your creative, intense, and sensitive child. Do you believe that your child can grow and improve with practice and hard work? Or that her personality and abilities are pretty well set? Second, you should remember that the mindset you use to parent and teach your child has a significant impact on the view or mindset she has about herself and thus affects how she feels about herself.

As Palladino points out, it is critical to "neutralize your thoughts" and "watch what you say" when you are with your child. This makes sense, since your mindset will influence what you are thinking about your child and what messages you communicate to him.

> *Taichi, age eight, just will not get ready in the morning. How many times do I have to remind him to get dressed for school? All he wants to do is play with his Lego sets or read his newest library book. How hard can it be to do simple things like get dressed and brush his teeth? Will I need to go to college with him to make sure he gets to class wearing shoes?*

The way Taichi's mother talks to him is important. It's natural to want to use the language like Taichi's mother when we feel frustrated. However, it would make a significant difference if this mother were to consider that her son's personal characteristics of being a Dreamer, Discoverer, or Dynamo have positive aspects as well. If she can focus on that, she may find herself more inclined to choose different words and behaviors that reflect a more mindful attitude which, instead of framing Taichi as scattered and distracted, "coaches" him to engage in different behaviors. What if she said this instead:

> *Taichi, I know playing with your Legos is way more interesting than making your bed and brushing your teeth. Let's get this boring stuff done so you'll have more time to do what you like to do.*

Although you might think that eight-year-old children should be able to do repetitive and mundane everyday tasks on their own, they often don't until the frontal lobes of their brain mature a bit more and they have more personal interest in being prepared for the day versus being drawn to the "shiny object" of their immediate interest.

A growth mindset will help you to approach your child in a positive, productive way as opposed to a negative, powerless way. When we believe that we can learn and improve with time and effort, and when we model that belief to our children, we can help them feel better about themselves and see themselves as "works in progress" rather than just a helpless mess with no hopes for changing the situation.

Offer Structured Flexibility

Structured flexibility is a term that emerged during our first summer of running a week-long overnight summer camp for bright, creative children. We had a daily schedule with specific activities offered at certain times and staff assigned to particular posts throughout the day. But we quickly discovered that while the kids in the program liked knowing what was to come during the day, they also wanted to have a voice in changing things as the day wore on.

We found ourselves naturally adapting to the children's requests within the larger structure of the camp, and that approach worked quite well for both the children and the adults who were in charge. To be fair, adapting is not always a choice! Creative children tend to demand change. They have strong opinions and form their own ideas about how things should be done. They bargain and negotiate like accomplished attorneys, or they simply just do what they want and ignore the rest.

Despite that, we as adults, and as parents, have a choice. We can rigidly hold to our schedules and rules and timelines, or we can adapt, give our children some choice and some freedom, and in doing so teach them to negotiate and compromise. Of course, there are some scheduled obligations that are non-negotiable, like school, extracurricular classes, sports, music lessons, tutoring, etc. But certainly there are other things that can be more flexible. One area for possible flexibility is during the moments that come between scheduled commitments:

> *Meena is 10. Whenever you are looking for her, just go wherever there are books; her head is always buried in them. She can go for a whole day without remembering to eat if she is immersed in another world through reading. She also loves playing the violin; however, she forgets to practice because she is always reading, and it's a struggle to get her out the door to her lessons. She doesn't seem to have any sense of time or really care that she could be making others wait for her.*

First, we should assume that Meena does care about others; creative children usually are very sensitive to the feelings of others. But Meena often is not aware of what is expected of her in the moment, or of the stress she is causing her parents, or of the impact she will have on her violin teacher if she is late. Why does she not think about the effects of her behavior? Because she is living in the moment, and the future has not yet arrived; the future is simply not in her awareness. After months of nagging and complaining, Meena's father decided to try a new approach:

> Dad: *Meena, we will be leaving for your violin lesson in one hour. It is time to start your homework so you can finish it before we go.*

Meena: *But I just got home from school. Can't I read and then do my homework after violin?*

Dad: *I wish I could say yes, but every time we've tried that, you haven't done it later.*

Meena: *I promise I will do it after. I just want to read now. I will do it after, I promise.*

Dad: *Okay, we can try this again, but if it doesn't work this time, we will have to come up with another plan.*

Does it feel like Meena's father is going nowhere? He clearly is taking a chance, knowing that Meena has tried this stalling tactic before. It's good that he's enforcing the overall structure of the day while still allowing Meena to have a say in the timing of events. But in this new scenario, he also has used different language and a different mindset. Remember our discussion on mindsets? Mindset control is evident in this example: the father communicated a willingness to let Meena do things her way in the hopes that she will succeed. He then introduced the idea of additional problem-solving that may be needed if Meena's plan doesn't work. Further, he spoke carefully so as not to make negative statements about Meena's previous inability to follow through on a plan. Meena has been given structured flexibility. It will be up to her to demonstrate whether or not she can work within the loose confines of that flexibility.

Give Choices Instead of Commands

Do you know anyone who likes to be told what to do? No? As you've likely noticed, intense and creative kids like to do things their own way and *really* don't like to be told what to do. Children, particularly bright, strong-willed children, like to feel as though they have a say in what happens to them and that their ideas count. It helps them to feel validated as important human beings when we allow them to have input into decisions that affect them. In addition, there is a much greater chance that they will go along with a plan that they have some sense of control over or that they buy into. Giving choices and allowing input is also consistent with the Nurturing Parent approach, which values and respects children as independent beings who have the ability to make decisions. It gives children a sense of autonomy and a chance to take on increasing responsibility for their actions and decisions.

As parents, we need our children to do certain things at certain times. However, we also need to teach them to be self-directed and responsible. Do we do this by telling them what to do, how to do it, and when to do it? That tends to create conflict and usually does not result in the desired outcome. Further, since your child is likely intense and strong-willed, it often results in him defying your requests or commands in order to preserve his sense of identity.

> *Jonah, 13, insists on doing things his way. He does not want to do anything that he cannot clearly see the reason for doing. He can argue for hours over why he shouldn't have to do something he doesn't want to do. One day, he decided that going to a family gathering was pointless because he had nothing to say to any of his relatives. He argued that all they do is ask him stupid questions that he doesn't want to answer. He wanted instead to stay home and play his guitar because he was writing a song. He felt that working on his music would be a better use of his time.*

This is a common dilemma, particularly for adolescents who find relating to family members uncomfortable and their own interests far more engaging and important. As a child becomes an adolescent, he needs more room to make decisions—or at least to feel as though he is making his own decisions. Jonah's mother found herself in a difficult situation when Jonah balked at going to the family get-together; if she forced him to go, she knew what would come next—a full-blown power struggle. How did she handle this situation? Here's what she said to him:

> *Jonah, I know you find our family gatherings at Grandma's house boring these days, but these events are important to us as Grandma gets older and more forgetful. We may not always have her with us. We have some flexibility with our visit today.*

You can go to Grandma's for part of the time and be home for part of the time. Would you rather go earlier and have free time later, or go later and work on your music now?

Jonah's mother knew that she would meet with opposition when she told her strong-willed son about the family's plans, so she found a way to give him a choice within the confines of a situation that was not negotiable. This allowed Jonah to have some control over his day and feel as though his feelings and interests mattered. An approach like this is often very effective for defusing an inevitable battle between child and parent.

Provide Consistent Boundaries

Despite their constant pushing and challenging, children actually want and need boundaries; they feel safe when they know the rules of acceptable behavior. While parenting creative children requires spontaneous flexibility, as Jonah's story so aptly illustrates, providing consistency about what is and what is not appropriate behavior is important for helping your child develop her own internal boundaries of behavior.

We have noted that one important characteristic of Nurturing Parents is that they help their children develop self-discipline and good judgment by giving them opportunities to make their own choices within certain limits. The older and more experienced a child gets at making good decisions, the more freedom she should have to practice using her judgment, and the fewer limits she should need. However, a child who demonstrates poor judgment will need her boundaries reinforced.

April, age 11, was left home alone while her mother went to the store. April is a creative child whose interests bounce from subject to subject with random abandon. Her current passion was making candles using melted wax. April's mother, knowing her daughter's obsession with the interest du jour, made sure to tell April to wait for her to get back before starting on her latest project. "I know, Mom!" April replied emphatically, and she meant it. All she planned to do was get everything ready.

April scoured the house for supplies and found an empty tin can in the garage. "A perfect container for melting the wax!" she thought. Before she knew it, the wax was in the can and on the stove. A few minutes later, while gathering up some different colored wax sticks from her bedroom, April smelled smoke coming from the kitchen. The stove was on fire, with flames engulfing the can of wax. Fortunately the fire diminished quickly on its own, but only after considerable damage to the stove.

This is an example of how a child's passion or drive to create can lead to behaviors that are seen as defiant. In April's case, she truly had planned to wait for her mother to return before beginning to make the candles, but her enthusiasm for the project ran away with her, and she was in trouble before she knew it. (Remember that at age 11, her brain isn't so good at using rational thinking processes yet.) April's lack of forethought led to what could have been a very dangerous situation. She had disobeyed her mother's orders and put herself—and her family's home—at great risk.

That evening, April's father came into her room to talk to her. Naturally, he was upset by the incident. He started by telling April that he was very happy that she was safe. He then asked her how things had unfolded and why she had not chosen to wait for her mother to come home. April had no good answers. Her father then stated that April would need to help pay for the cleaning and repairs to the kitchen, and she would not be able to stay home alone for a while in order to rebuild her parents' trust.

"For how long?" April asked, dismayed.

"I don't know yet," her father answered. "Your mother and I need to think about it for a day or two. What happened was very serious, and we're glad you weren't hurt, but we need to make sure you understand how important it is to follow the rules we set for you."

April's father did several things right in this scenario. First, he remained calm in a situation that was potentially very emotional. (It could have easily turned into an angry shouting match with tears and yelling, but thanks to Dad's calm demeanor, the conversation stayed reasonable.) Next, he set tighter limits on April's freedoms since she had not shown the responsibility needed to make good decisions when left home alone. He also emphasized the notion of trust, an important value that was breached. And finally, he modeled the need for processing information and not reacting immediately to a situation by telling April that he and her mother would discuss possible consequences further. A good follow-up, after things calmed down, would be to ask April what she learned from the experience and what she might do differently next time.

Use Natural and Logical Consequences versus Punishment

The distinction between consequences and punishment is important. Although both are meant to teach a lesson, our experience shows that consequences that naturally and logically follow from a behavior are often far more effective for teaching a child responsibility than punishing the child by arbitrarily taking something away. Bright, creative kids often need to understand the reasoning behind an action in order to internalize it. They often will resist punishments that seem punitive or that do not make sense to them. For April, not being allowed to stay home alone for a few weeks as a logical consequence of setting the stove on fire makes more sense than taking away her cell phone privileges or not permitting her to go out with her friends. Those punishments impact her social life but have no connection to the trust her parents need to have in her before she can stay at home alone again.

Just as the term implies, a natural or logical consequence is a natural or logical result of the undesirable action or behavior. Let's say a child rides his bicycle without a helmet, which goes against the rules his parents have set for him. A logical consequence would be to limit him from riding his bike until he learns to put his helmet on. A natural consequence would be a bump on his head and a headache when he falls off his bike. In a case like this, parents may not want to go with the natural consequence because not wearing a helmet could be dangerous, and the child needs to know that. (Remember that Nurturing Parents protect their children from harm.) A logical consequence would ensure the child's safety while also tying the consequence to the prohibited action. In contrast, a punishment would be to take away the child's video games for the day. But there is nothing in that disciplinary measure that links it to a message of safety. When an issue is important and parents want to establish a clear boundary, they might firmly say, "You must always wear a helmet if you want to ride your bike; it's a matter of safety; there is no negotiating."

The word *discipline* comes from the Latin root *disciple*, which means "to teach." Natural or logical consequences as a form of discipline make sense to children and have a better chance of teaching the lessons you want to them to learn than punishments. The goal of Nurturing Parents is to teach children, not to punish them.

Another important reason for consistently using natural and logical consequences is that doing so helps to make children accountable for their behaviors. If you do not give your child a consequence for breaking rules, you are limiting his learning opportunities. You know how fast your child's mind works and how it drifts off into another world of imagination and creation. How can he learn if he is not held accountable and does not have to think about his behavior for longer than the moment he is being yelled at?

> *"When can I ride my bike again? It's been forever!" Bryan pleaded for the tenth time in half an hour.*
>
> *"You can tomorrow," his mother said, "after you have had time to think about how important it is to wear a helmet and how important safety rules are."*

Of course, there are times when your child really misbehaves and you think you just can't take it anymore! Punishments can be helpful in more extreme situations and when you really want your child to know that he has crossed a very important line. An example is when a child becomes violent with you or your property or engages in unsafe behavior, either knowingly or unknowingly. Most of us would consider a punishment or a grounding justifiable in this kind of situation. We suggest, however, that punishments are the exception rather than the rule and that natural and logical consequences are the best way for teaching a child appropriate behavior.

Pick Your Battles

In his book *The Explosive Child*, Ross Green (2010) talks about how parents are the experts on their child's behavior and therefore know how to both promote and avoid a meltdown. Whether you have a Dreamer, Discoverer, or Dynamo, your child likely gives you several opportunities a day to remind her of something she is not doing that you asked her to do, how she doesn't seem to be taking others' feelings into account, or how she is overreacting when she doesn't get her way. Parenting these kids can be exhausting. You may find yourself waking up each morning preparing for battle and going to bed each night after a long siege of getting them to bed.

You must remember how much control you actually *do* have in setting the tone of your relationship with your child. It may not often seem like it, but always remember that you can choose whether to: (1) get upset about your child's behavior, (2) engage in a power struggle, (3) let it go, or (4) help your child complete a particular task. Do you want to yell at her every time she gets lost in her room playing with her stuffed animals or continues reading when you have asked her to bring you her laundry or get dressed for soccer? Knowing as you do that she is apt to get side-tracked when you make this kind of request, you might avoid a battle by making your request and then checking on her in five minutes to remind her, or even going into her room to help her with the task. With creative children, who tend to be very strong-willed and also so focused on the task at hand to the exclusion of all else, there is a potential battle around every corner. You need to choose on the very few situations that are worth a fight, and work hard to let the others go.

Focus on Your Child's Strengths

We saved this point for last, as it cannot be overstated. We all rely on our strengths for our jobs and our relationships. We do our best to avoid our weak areas and to reduce the possibility of our weaknesses negatively affecting our job performance and our relationships. Earlier in the chapter, we gave Palladino's examples of seeing a divergent, creative child's behavior through a strength-based perspective versus a pathology or problem-based perspective. Do you want to choose to focus on your child's inattentiveness, distractibility, and impulsiveness or on the creative, imaginative, and risk-taking behaviors that are responsible for his remarkable inventions?

The answer is obvious. Of course you want to concentrate on his strengths, yet we live in a society that tends to focus on what's wrong with a person rather than what's right, what needs fixing rather than what is working well. However, keep in mind that not all adults can adopt a positive perspective with their creative child. Creative children often do need some guidance and support in learning to "play the game" or "jump through the hoops" of school and to focus on the task at hand.

As you probably well know, creative children are at risk for getting negative feedback from parents, teachers, and peers for doing things differently, or not doing things not at all. It is critical to support and highlight their strengths, whether those are in music, sports, storytelling, leadership, or painting. It is imperative that your child internalize his strengths—that he knows what he is good at—so he can feel self-confident as he forms his identity. We want our children to internalize more messages that start with "I am good at…" than ones that start with "I am bad at…." We want them to have a mindset that promotes working hard to accomplish tasks by knowing that they have the ability and resources to do so.

Boosting—and Nurturing—Creative Potential

As we have noted, nurturing parents—including those parents who strive to boost creativity in their children—do not always find it easy, yet it can still be very rewarding. Being a nurturing parent—with the intent to boost creative potential—calls for an incredible amount of self-restraint, patience, compromise, negotiation, and trust in yourself and your child. Among all of the parenting styles that have been described, we believe that being a Nurturing parent is best when raising creative children. These children need to feel that they are heard, trusted, and respected as individuals, and need to have a strong role in the decisions that affect their lives. However, if they are going to be productive, responsible, and compassionate individuals with a strong sense of self, they still need us to set limits and boundaries and to give consequences for their behavior when it is clearly out of bounds or hurtful. These children need our guidance while they are preoccupied with finding their own identities, developing their creativity, and discovering their place in the world.

We have yet to write about specific strategies for helping your creative, divergent-thinking child become more convergent—i.e., more organized, more focused on the task at hand, and better able to achieve goals. The Nurturing Parent approach provides the paradigm by which to parent your creative child. Our next chapter provides strategies for helping Dreamers, Discoverers, and Dynamos add some skills of convergence, planning, organizing, and focus to their highly developed divergent abilities so they can better bring their creative endeavors to fruition.

Chapter 10
Creative Ways to Build Executive Functions

We now know that if you tried to be creative using only the [divergent capacities]...of your brain, it'd be like living with ideas perpetually at the tip of your tongue, just beyond reach.

~ Bronson & Merryman[74]

By now, it should be no surprise to you when we say that creative and divergent-thinking children—kids who have imaginations that are literally out of this world—often have difficulty following specific directions, planning for schedules and times, performing well in school, and finishing projects that they start. We have provided many descriptions of creative children and teens who have extraordinary imaginations and divergent thinking skills but who also struggle with planning and organizing abilities. The goal then seems to be to raise a creative child in a flexible environment that supports risk taking, innovation, but which also engenders responsibility, dependability, and the capacity to follow through with the necessary tasks and obligations of home life and school life.

This is perhaps the greatest challenge of raising a creative child—to provide and maintain a flexible and spontaneous environment while at the same time helping the child develop essential life skills—specifically, executive functioning skills—like organization and planning. We have presented and supported a parenting style that honors creativity and individuality, but which also acknowledges the need to support creative children in developing the skills and abilities necessary for being responsible, following through, and developing positive coping skills throughout life.

Brain Development and Executive Functioning

Earlier in the book, we described different aspects of brain development, including the parts of our brain called the frontal lobes or prefrontal cortex, often referred to as the "CEO" of the brain. Our frontal lobes are responsible for a number of organizational and planning abilities known collectively as *executive functioning*. Interestingly, research has shown that the brighter the child, the slower these functions tend to develop.[75] As a result, it is common for creative and divergent thinkers to have weaknesses in their organizational, planning, and decision-making skills. Here are a few examples of some everyday executive functioning breakdowns that may sound familiar to you:

- *Why do I have to remind you to brush your teeth... feed the dog... hang up your bath towel... turn off the computer... put dishes in the sink... do your homework?*
- *Listen to me for a minute, and then you can go back to your project. Did you hear what I just said?*

- *I can't see the floor in your room. How do you find anything in here? What do you mean you can't find your homework? Can you please clean up this project before you start the next one?*

Executive functioning skills are important in everyday life, at home, in school, and in the world of work. We need them to complete projects and follow through with the development of creative ideation. However, we are not born with these skills. Infants do not have executive functioning abilities. They cry when they are hungry and sleep when they are tired. Similarly, toddlers don't have much in the way of executive functioning skills either. In fact, it's normal for them to go through the "terrible twos," during which they have regular emotional meltdowns, make messes, and engage in impulsive behaviors like drawing on walls or throwing things. It is our job as parents to both keep our children safe and nurture their growth by teaching the organizational, planning, and decision-making skills that they will need throughout their lives. For our purposes, we will refer to this set of skills as *executive planning skills*. Many creative children function very well, yet many of them would benefit from improved planning and organization skills.

Ideally, we as parents support our children as they acquire competence in their executive planning skills; then, as they grow, they should gradually begin taking on executive functioning tasks on their own. We expect them to learn to clean up after themselves, get dressed on their own, organize their surroundings, think about what might be dangerous, remember their schedules and responsibilities, and control their emotions when they get upset. But that doesn't always happen the way we want it to, and while children who lack executive planning skills can be difficult to parent at home, their deficits in these skill areas can be especially problematic at school.

Children generally are given a great deal of support in areas like planning and organization through second grade. But by third grade, they are expected to take on more responsibility for being organized and keeping track of their assignments. With each passing year, the expectation for independence and self-management increases, going to higher levels in middle school, then high school, and finally college, where time management is essential to success.

No matter their age or grade level, without specific intervention and support, our wonderfully creative and brilliantly imaginative children often have difficulty sustaining attention in class, organizing materials, completing assignments, and turning them in on time. Further, because of their divergent thinking style, they are strong on understanding the context or the "big picture" of the subject matter at hand yet weak at memorizing specific details and dates, which are very often important in the current test-driven environments of many schools. Many creative children also have trouble planning the steps in sequence for what needs to occur to bring a project to completion. They need assistance with this, and one of the best ways to help is through a process sometimes referred to as *scaffolding*.

The notion of scaffolding is an important concept that you can use in several aspects of parenting and supporting your child's growth. Just think of scaffolding around a building. The scaffolding allows workers to reach a level in the building that wouldn't be possible without the support. Once the work is done and the building is secure, the scaffolding can be removed. Scaffolding in parenting is the same. It is the process of supporting your child's growth by helping her in ways that allow her to achieve until she can learn to implement those supportive measures on her own. An example of this is modeling the various steps in a task for a young child to imitate, or setting up a calendar with alerts on your adolescent's smart phone, rather than just expecting her to remember all of her activities and schoolwork due dates. Once the child learns the steps of the task, or the teen learns how to manage her time so that her work is completed before it's due, parents can step back a bit, allowing the child to use her newly mastered skills without the aid of the scaffolding.

So how do you help your child develop executive planning skills so that you don't have to act as her frontal lobes for the rest of her life? We will offer practical strategies for improving those skills in your child, but before we do, we would like to talk a little more about executive planning skills so that you are equipped with the knowledge you need to tackle the challenge of building these abilities in your creative child.

Eleven Essential Executive Planning Skills

There is another book we'd like you to know about. It's called *Smart but Scattered* by Peg Dawson, Ed.D. and Richard Guare, Ph.D. (2009) who have extensive experience working with children who have executive functioning weaknesses. In the book, Dawson and Guare outline 11 executive planning skills along two dimensions that relate to our "thinking" and "doing."

The executive planning skills related to *thinking* include:

1. *Working memory*—the ability to hold information in your head and use information from the past when determining how to act in the present or future. "*The principal talked to me last week about running in the hall, so I should remember not to run when we're going out to recess.*"
2. *Planning/prioritization*—the ability to plot a strategy for doing something, as well as the ability to determine what is most important versus what is less important in that process. "*I have to do my homework and practice the piano, but I want to text my friends about our plans for this weekend. I have two hours until I have to go to drama class. How should I plan my time?*"
3. *Organization*—the ability to make a system for completing a project, which includes a way to track progress. "*I like to make lists of things I need to do. It makes me feel good to be able to cross them off when I've completed them. I make sure to put deadlines on the list so I can track when things need to be done.*"
4. *Time management*—understanding the concept of time and how to use segments of time to complete a task or goal. "*I know it will take more than an hour to study for the math test tomorrow, so I'm starting my study time earlier than usual.*"
5. *Metacognition*—the ability to think about your thinking. It involves taking a step back and thinking about your behavior and its impact on others, as well as how well you are doing at meeting your goals. *"I've been worried about how I'm going to do on the AP exams. It bothered me all week until I thought*

about it and realized that I've studied as much as I can—I'm just nervous. But now, instead of focusing on that, I'm reminding myself that I'm as prepared as I'm ever going to be, and I'm just going to do the best I can."

The executive planning skills involved in *behavior* include:

6. *Response inhibition*—the ability to think before you act. It involves holding back impulses and considering the impact of your behaviors before doing anything. "*I caught myself and decided not to shout back to the girl who teased me about my curly hair. That just would have started an argument and made a scene.*"

7. *Emotional control*—the ability to manage your emotions and thereby control your behaviors. "*I was getting angry that my teacher kept changing the due date for our history reports. I wanted to say something about how frustrated I was, but I really want to be this teacher's teaching assistant. So I decided not to argue with him about it in order to show my teacher that I can be mature and am ready for responsibility.*"

8. *Sustained attention*—the ability to maintain attention and resist distraction, even when bored or tired. "*My teacher insists on talking without letting us have any class discussion about the topic she's presenting. When she's going on and on in class, I find my mind wandering. But I've learned that if I take notes on what she's saying, it helps me stay focused, and that way I don't miss anything that I'll need to know for the test.*"

9. *Task initiation*—the ability to start a project or assignment without excessive avoidance or procrastination. The adage "How do you eat an elephant? One bite at a time" applies here. Since creative children are "big picture" thinkers, they have the capacity to envision fantastic projects and creations, but they may have great difficulty knowing where to begin or how to make a plan for the series of steps which will take them through the development and production of their ideas. As a result, some of them never even manage to get started. "*I*

knew I needed to write down the steps for each part of the volcano project I'm going to do for science class. Once I had a plan for what I needed to do, I was able to start doing a few things each day on the project."

10. *Goal-directed persistence*—the ability to continue working on a defined task, make progress, resist distractions, and see the project through to completion. "*Even though it's spring break and prom is coming up, I'm still making time to work on my piano piece every day so I'll be ready for the recital in two weeks.*"

11. *Flexibility*—the ability to alter what you do or how you do it when it's necessary to do so. Creative children often are innately flexible when it comes to their own thinking, planning, or projects. They naturally think in terms of "Ooooh, I could do this, or *this,* or *THIS!*" New ideas and options can be very compelling and intrinsically rewarding. However, when there is a change in external circumstances requiring flexibility, those same creative children may become irritated and even stubborn. The ability to revise plans based on new information or to change or alter behavior based on mistakes, unforeseen circumstances, or changing conditions is an ability that creative children may need adult support to achieve.

    "I had been waiting all week for the aluminum I ordered online to complete my Iron Man suit. When the box finally arrived, I opened it up to find a soft metal mesh instead of the aluminum sheets I had ordered. But the costume contest was only a week away, so I didn't have time to return it and get what I really wanted. Boy, was I disappointed! But I got to thinking that the metal mesh would sure make a good suit of chainmail, and I ended up making an awesome medieval outfit instead. And it turns out that three other kids were dressed as Iron Man anyway, so it worked out great!"

Goodness of Fit

As you can see, there are several different abilities or skill sets that are involved in becoming a self-directed and independent person. Perhaps you were taking an inventory of your own skills in each of the areas as you read through the 11 items on the list. We hope so, since the next thing you need to do is to assess your own executive skill strengths and weaknesses. How your strengths and weaknesses in those areas match up to your child's can have a positive or a negative impact on your child's functioning, as well as on your relationship. This is a concept called "goodness of fit."

Parents who have executive planning weaknesses similar to their child's often see the child's weaker behaviors as less problematic than do parents who have executive strengths in the areas of their child's weaknesses. Thus, the parent who is good at planning ahead will be more upset with a child who doesn't seem able to plan ahead than will the parent who doesn't plan ahead well herself. For example, a mother who doesn't plan ahead for meals may have to constantly run to the store to get ingredients for dinner. This is normal behavior for her. In turn, she may not make much of a fuss when her child waits until the last minute to mention that a project is due tomorrow and that he needs to get to the store for posterboard and paint.

It's not hard to understand why the parent with the same executive planning weaknesses as the child may not be the best parent to teach the child those skills. Logically, the parent who is strong in executive planning skills may be best suited to teach those skills; however, that parent has a greater likelihood of becoming frustrated with the lack of those skills in the child. When this occurs, there is a high chance for conflict that can interfere with both learning and the parent-child relationship. "Why didn't you think about the posterboard before now? You say you've actually known about this project for more than a week? I'm so disappointed in you! I really resent having to give up my evening to take you to get posterboard, especially when we were just out that way yesterday! I hope you never do this again!"

So as you can see, taking inventory of your own executive planning strengths and weaknesses is important in helping you consider which of your child's skills truly need work. If you are fortunate, your child's other parent (or another important adult in the child's life, including grandparents or aunts and uncles, or perhaps even a good family friend) will have strengths in executive planning skills that are your weak areas, and that person can help to improve your child's executive weaknesses.

We are not saying that if you have an executive planning weakness, you can't teach your child that skill. On the contrary. In fact, the best plan is for you to identify your skills and abilities so that you can work on your weaker ones yourself and at the same time teach your child. If you know that your child is weak in areas such as organization and planning, a proactive approach often works best. You might say: "Since we both have difficulty remembering what we need to do for important deadlines, let's be sure we check your backpack every night to see what long-term assignments or projects might be coming up. Then we can get any supplies ahead of time and make a list of things we have to do. That way we won't be rushed trying to finish a big project at the last minute."

Bright, creative kids love learning with their parents, and as we discussed in the parenting chapter, they appreciate honesty and authenticity. You don't need to be perfect, just human. And remember, modeling values such as bettering yourself—in this case improving your own organization and planning skills—and being honest about your strengths and weaknesses are key components to effectively raising creative children.

Making a Plan

Now that you have determined which executive skills you and your child may be strong or weak in, you can design a support plan for your child. You will want to target a specific thinking or behavior skill and design a plan to successfully improve that skill. We have seen time and time again that the most well-intentioned support plans don't work because there really is no clear plan! Instead, there is a strong desire for a child to "grow up, get with the program, and try harder," with the primary approach unfortunately reverting to yelling and repeating the same things over and over. It is all too easy to slip into this timeless, ineffective parenting technique—we've done it plenty of times ourselves, and we have a professional background in this!

The first step in making a plan is to go back to the list of 11 skill sets to determine which executive planning skills your child needs support in developing. If you are finding that he is weak in several skills, try to remember that he is not yet grown up, and you still have time to help teach and guide him. On the other hand, you might be pleasantly surprised to find that your child has executive planning strengths that you did not realize he had. But even if he only has one identified strength, we strongly recommend that you capitalize on it. We have found that successful people do what they are good at well and then find balance by getting help for their weaker areas. It is very important to highlight your child's strengths and use them wherever possible while identifying and teaching to his executive planning weaknesses.

Once you have identified an area or areas that you feel need additional support, list them in order of priority. Remember, we want your approach to be effective, which means it has to be manageable for you and your child. Once you have put them in order, we suggest you focus on the top one or two identified categories or behaviors that need improvement.

In the sections that follow, we discuss the executive planning skills described by Dawson and Guare and include their suggestions for improving your child's skills in each of the areas. We have used these recommendations for years in working with creative children and their parents and have found them to be quite effective.

Enhance Working Memory, The Gateway to Attention

Working memory refers to the ability to hold information in one's head while carrying out multi-step tasks. Children with strong working memories are better able to stay focused on the task at hand than those with poor working memories, are not as easily distractible, and are more successful in school. The following strategies can help your child enhance this important skill:

- *Look into your child's eyes when asking or reminding her to do something.* Remember, your creative child is often in her own world, mentally involved in something important to her at the moment. She needs focused attention to process your request. It is also helpful to ask her to repeat back what you've just said.
- *Keep external distractions to a minimum.* This speaks to environmental engineering. It is important to provide your child with an environment that increases opportunities for processing and remembering information—especially when the child is not inherently interested and engaged in the activity. Remove more exciting or novel stimuli, and keep noises to a minimum. However, keep in mind that this is an approach to support your child in completing a necessary task. It does not apply to the free play of creative activity, in which complexity and variety are welcome.
- *Use written and visual reminders.* Most of us rely on visual reminders such as lists, Post-its, and memos on our smart phones. Your child can use these kinds of reminders as well. Young children benefit from pictures or other visuals of the tasks they need to complete. For older children, maximize the use of technology such as text reminders and electronic calendars. Teach your child to set reminders on her phone rather than expecting her to remember something she likely won't.
- *Rehearse and practice what to remember in particular situations.* Sometimes children simply don't know what they should be trying to remember in the first place. If this is the case, you can role play with your child different scenarios in which you focus on what specifically needs to be remembered among the barrage of information to which she's exposed. For example, you could pretend to read off instructions for a class project. In your example, include several nonessential points, as well as some important ones, like what the topic is allowed to be about, how many resources the student must use for research, and the date the project is due. Then see if

the child can remember the significant points and discuss with her why they are significant.

- *Help your child develop visual strategies for remembering specific information.* One way of doing this is to have your child visualize her bedroom. She then imagines placing particular objects in different locations in her room—but those "objects" are instead bits of information that she needs to be able to recall later. The child can think of "where" she put that "item," allowing her to evoke the memory of the specific piece of information she needs. For example, perhaps she can associate her Monday cello lessons with a family picture taken at the symphony that sits on her top shelf. When she looks at the photo, she remembers that she will have cello on Monday. The key is that the "places" and the connection of the fact or activity with those places need to meaningful to your child.

Teach Planning and Prioritizing

Planning and prioritizing refer to being able to make a plan to achieve an end goal, deciding which components are more important or need to be completed first, and making decisions along the way that result in achieving the goal. Here are some suggestions for improving this executive skill in your child:

- *Teach your child at an early age to make plans.* Model planning skills by making statements like, "Now let's see, what should I do first? I think I will make a list and then decide what is most important." Make sure your child sees you making specific plans that result in noticeable achievements, even if they're minor. For example, redecorating a room, preparing a holiday meal, or organizing a yard sale all involve planning to successfully complete.

- *Involve your child in the process of making plans.* This will increase both your child's skill at planning and his engagement in the process. Use an activity that he will be motivated to become involved in, such as planning an outing of his choice or building a project or invention. "Okay, what supplies do we need? Where should we get them? How long do you think it will take us to do this?"

- *Teach prioritization by asking your child what needs to be done first.* "Which step here is the most important? In what order do you think you should do this?" If you disagree, ask him why he thinks the way he does. Either he will surprise you with his creative logic, or you can discuss why a different step might make more sense.

Foster Organization

Organization refers to the ability to establish and maintain a system for arranging and keeping track of important items. Some suggestions for improving your child's organizational skills include:

- *Devise an organizational system.* With your child, put together a system in which she can stay organized in key areas: backpack, desk, room, art studio, workshop. Find out what will work for her, whether it is needing to see her things or having them put away and out of sight. Determine what supports, such as folders, boxes, or baskets, may be helpful. Creative children will get on board—often with surprising enthusiasm—with getting organized if their organizational system includes color-coded folders or see-through boxes where they actually can see their stuff, even when it's put away. Decide on regular times when your child will engage in specific organizational behaviors, such as organizing her backpack before bedtime on school nights, or picking up and putting away supplies in her art studio every Sunday night after a weekend of working on projects there.

- *Supervise the system.* This is key. Putting a system in place is not enough—yet. Support your child's growth and development by supervising her and providing coaching and companionship as she works at keeping organized. However, do not straighten up, pick up, clean up, or organize for your child without her present! Provide the structure and guidance to help her internalize the plan, and then see that it works.

Encourage Time Management

Time management involves understanding the concept of time, determining how long a task will take, and completing the task within the amount of time allotted. Ideas for improving your child's time management skills include:

- *Maintain a schedule that balances routine and predictability with flexibility.* Maintaining some regular routines helps your child understand what happens when, as well as how long things generally take. Examples include having morning and bedtime rituals and doing homework at a particular time of the day. Then, when those necessary tasks are done, time is freed up for choice activities and pursuit of your child's creative passions.
- *Teach time estimation by talking to your child about how long things take.* You can integrate this into the suggestions for planning and prioritizing. Help your child estimate the amount of time that various tasks will take—whether it's completing homework or working on a design for a soapbox derby car—and then add them up to determine how long he needs to complete all of his tasks or chores.
- *Teach backward planning.* Help your child make a plan based on a due date and what needs to happen before then. For example, your child's Shakespeare project is due in one month. Help him make a list of all the things he needs to do to create his project, break those items down into individual steps, and predict about how long each step will take. It is also important to teach your child to build in extra time for the unexpected, in case things take longer than planned (as they often do). The goal is for your child to have the experience of completing a project without undue stress and last-minute drama so he can see the value in planning and organization.
- *Use calendars and schedules.* Visually blocking out time on a calendar teaches your child about how much time actually is available in each day and how to structure his tasks in

reasonable and reality-based time periods. Using different colors for different activities works well with most creative children's visual styles and aesthetic leanings.

Cultivate Metacognition

Metacognition is the ability to think about one's thinking. It involves the ability to be self-aware and reflective and to monitor one's behavior. Here are some suggestions for improving your child's ability to evaluate her own performance or behavior:

- *Provide specific feedback.* Creative children respond well to feedback and comments that are specifically geared toward particular elements of their work or behavior. "I like how you put detail in every flower." "You did a nice job of putting your books back in your backpack before starting to play on the computer."
- *Teach your child to evaluate her performance by asking her questions about what she thinks.* The best way to teach your child to think about her work or behavior is to ask her questions about it instead of commenting on it yourself. "How do you think you did on your test?" "Do you like the way your essay turned out?" "How do you think your teacher is going to respond to your illustration?" It is okay to offer some suggestions for improvement, but do your best not to be judgmental or to impose your own standards on the task. It is best if your child feels ownership and satisfaction in her work.
- *Have your child describe what the finished product will look like or what it means in advance.* Make sure she understands what it means to clean her room, do her homework, and spend time studying. What all is involved? What needs to be done first, next, and last? Ask her to explain what actions she will take to complete the task. This gets her consciously thinking about what she will do and why.
- *Teach your child a set of questions that she can ask herself when she is working on or is done with a project.* Self-evaluation is

a helpful tool that children can use to consider their work. Teach your child to ask questions like "How am I doing?" "Am I sticking to my plan?" "How does it look?" "Did I do everything I was supposed to?"

As we've discussed, creative children tend to be highly sensitive to their surroundings, to others, and to their own emotions. To help your child improve her understanding of her emotions, as well as her ability to read others' emotions and cues in social situations, we suggest the following:

- *Play games trying to guess what people are thinking or feeling based on their body language or facial expressions.* Ask your child to guess what you are feeling or thinking based on how your face looks. You also can turn off the sound when watching television shows or movies and ask your child to guess what the characters are feeling.
- *Help your child identify types of tones—teasing, sarcastic, pleased, angry, etc.* Have your child practice paying attention to changes in your tone of voice and determining what the different pitches or tones suggests about how you may be feeling. Teach her about subtle facial clues or body language that suggest a person is happy, mad, or sad. What happens to the person's eyes, mouth, or shoulders?
- *Ask your child to predict how her actions may make someone else feel in advance, before she engages in the behavior.* It helps for children to think about how their actions look to others. In some instances, more objective realizations that come from this exercise may help a child to change her behavior completely.

Build Response Inhibition

Simply put, response inhibition refers to the ability to think before acting. As we all know, it's important to be able to think a situation through before acting on our initial knee-jerk reactions. Some strategies for helping your child increase his response inhibition include:

- *Help your child learn to delay gratification.* In our immediate-gratification society, children (and adults) are used to getting what they want immediately, but that doesn't teach the values of patience and contemplation. Purposefully make your child wait a short time before responding to his requests. "I will get out the art supplies after I finish making my shopping list." Increase the wait time as your child gets older. This teaches him to accept delay.
- *Have your child earn something he wants.* You can have your child work toward a goal by engaging in a desired behavior such as keeping his room organized for a week. Then on the weekend, celebrate with a family fieldtrip of his choosing. This is a form of delayed gratification, but it specifically rewards purposeful behavior.
- *Prepare your child for situations that require impulse control.* Talk through a situation before entering it. "There will be a lot of kids on the playground, and there won't be enough toys for everyone. It will be important to take turns and share." Giving your child notice of a potential problem in advance allows him to think about what he will do before he has an opportunity to act.
- *Practice response inhibition through role play.* Sometimes it helps children if you can practice or "rehearse" common situations in which they might feel inclined toward impulsive behavior. Your child can act as himself or as an imaginary child of his choosing, and you can pretend to be another child, or you might choose to take on the role of your child. One of you gets to approach the other and do something inappropriate, like take a toy from him or say something mean to him. Then you and your child can act out how to handle the situation, modeling restraint and consideration of the event before reacting in a negative manner. Praise your child for his creative and appropriate responses.

- *Set up an external reward system to reinforce impulse control.* Using a sticker chart or a similar age-appropriate visual aid for tracking performance works well for some children. This may sound counterintuitive, given that we have said numerous times that external rewards are creativity killers. However, there is a distinct difference between rewarding creativity and rewarding appropriate behavior. You can use external rewards to help motivate your child to manage his behavior by rewarding him for engaging in desired behaviors over a set period of time—for example, "You will get a star every day that you remember to bring your homework assignment papers home. When you've done that for two weeks, we can celebrate by going to a movie of your choice."

Improve Emotional Self-Control

Emotional control refers to the ability to manage and modulate one's emotions in order to successfully respond to the situation at hand, as well as to manage one's behaviors in varied contexts. Some useful strategies for improving your child's emotional control include:

- *Regulate and structure the environment.* Although creative children often seek novelty, they also benefit from structure and predictability. Daily routines reduce the amount of "surprises" and unexpected transitions that can be the cause of meltdowns.

- *Prepare your child by talking about what to expect in the coming situation, and discuss strategies for managing her feelings if she starts to get overwhelmed.* We discussed the first part of this strategy (preparing your child for what to expect) in the section on response inhibition. The latter part of this suggestion focuses on helping your child manage her strong emotions if she is not able to keep them at bay, despite her efforts to proactively thwart them. You can help your child develop a coping strategy "toolbox," which may include deep breathing, taking self-imposed timeouts, talking herself through a situation (i.e., self-talk), and reframing a situation in order to see it from another possible perspective.

Strengthen Sustained Attention

Sustained attention refers to the ability to keep paying attention despite being distracted, bored, or tired. Some recommendations to help your child strengthen his capacity to maintain his attention include:

- *Provide supervision or companionship.* Many children find it beneficial to have a parent present to watch them successfully complete a task, especially if what they're doing or working on is a weak area for them. For example, you might have to walk with your child into the bathroom to make sure he brushes his teeth before he goes to bed. Or you may need to sit with him and talk together while he cleans his room. This type of supervision or accompaniment may be necessary for longer than you might expect, but it will result in task completion and a lot less conflict than later arguing over what isn't finished. It is important not to be angry while accompanying your child in these activities, but to simply act neutral. You are there to see that the task gets done, and that is all.
- *Gradually increase attentional capacity.* Set a time period for how long your child will engage in a task such as homework or doing a chore. "I will set the timer for 10 minutes, and then you can take a break." Gradually increase the time as your child ages and/or shows the ability to sustain attention for longer periods of time.
- *Make the task more interesting.* Always try to make tasks more fun and interesting to increase your child's engagement. For example, if getting him to clean his room is a struggle, stimulate his creativity by having the toys talk as they are being put away, which can help make the task more fun. For older children, talk about subjects of interest with them while engaging in tasks they consider boring.
- *Celebrate sustained attention.* Motivate your child to improve this skill with an external reward or an activity of his choosing. Again, you're not rewarding creativity, but rather a specific behavior that will help him bring his creative ideas to fruition,

in addition to being a valuable asset in virtually every setting in which he'll find himself throughout his life.

Teach Task Initiation

Task initiation is the ability to start a task or project in a timely manner, which can be especially difficult for creative children who have so many ideas in their head that they can't decide which one to choose and therefore ultimately end up stalled before they even begin. Or they dream up ideas so grandiose that they couldn't fathom where to begin creating them. Here are some recommendations for helping your child learn this skill:

- *Provide visual cues for task initiation.* This is essentially the same recommendation we made for enhancing working memory. Set up reminders for your child, or better, make sure she knows how to set them for herself, by writing notes, sticking Post-its to her mirror or computer, or setting text alerts on her phone so that she will remember what needs to be done and when.
- *Break big tasks into small parts.* Recall how to eat an elephant? One bite at a time? Help your child manage feeling overwhelmed and get started by learning to do just one thing at a time. "Let's look at what's involved in your school project. First, you need to decide on a topic. Then you'll need to figure out what materials you'll need to gather in order to do it. Let's make a list so you can see everything you need to do and will be able to get started checking things off that list."
- *Help your child make a plan for accomplishing a task, including the cues or reminders that will be used.* You will increase the chances of success and engagement from your child if she plays a part in making the plan. Try to allow her to come up with strategies, and let her own them as much as possible. Of course, you may have to guide the process and make suggestions so that the plan can be carried out successfully.
- *Celebrate task initiation with a choice activity.* Are you noticing a pattern? Systems of rewards are useful for motivating

children to perform all kinds of positive behaviors. And the best rewards aren't monetary or "things"; they're events or even just time spent doing something pleasurable. "You've got half your homework done. Let's take a 20-minute break and bake some cookies now."

Support Goal-Directed Persistence

Simply stated, goal-directed persistence is working on a goal without getting unduly side-tracked. For creative children who may have several different ideas or projects that they're working on simultaneously, it can be difficult to focus on any one of them for long enough to carry it through to completion. The following suggestions can help your child increase persistence:

- *Provide your young child with small tasks that can be completed with some ease.* Examples include taking out the trash or feeding the family pet. Give positive feedback to your child for completing the task. Rather than a generic "Good job!" saying "Thank you" or "I appreciate that you did that" connects the child's follow-through to your initial request. The goal is to help your child internalize what it feels like to complete a task that is not necessarily of his own choosing and to derive satisfaction from having done so.

- *Allow your child to have choice in his goals, as he will be more intrinsically motivated to complete tasks in those situations.* It is important to capitalize on your child's interests when working on all of the executive planning skills. A child who enjoys what he's doing or can find some element of interest in it will be more motivated to adopt that skill and use it.

- *Provide your child with an incentive or reward that awaits him after he completes the task.* Once again, reinforcement of a desired behavior is key to successfully improving a skill. Some people think this is bribing, when in reality it is teaching the child about some aspects of how the world works. Incentives are used regularly to motivate people to complete tasks that are not intrinsically motivating.

- *Increase the amount of time your child must spend to complete a task.* Help your child to stay focused on a task for longer and longer periods of time by gradually increasing the amount of time you expect him to work on it. This builds his endurance or persistence for activities that are required but which are not necessarily inherently rewarding.
- *Provide reminders of the "big picture" or end result.* Creative children often think in terms of the bigger picture, but sometimes they can get caught up in the details too. It can be helpful to have a visual of the end product or result. "Remember, you only need to earn $10 more to get your Lego set."
- *Technology can be helpful for improving task persistence.* Especially with older children, using the alert feature on their phone or an electronic calendar on their computer can provide the structure needed to carry out a task like homework.

Encourage Flexibility

When we discuss flexibility within the framework of executive planning skills, we are not referring to creative children's innate tendency toward flexible thinking. Instead, we are referring to the flexibility necessary to change one's behavior or plans based on an unexpected change, obstacle, setback, or mistake. In that context, flexibility is required in response to outside circumstances—those over which we have no control. It is at just such times that creative children—who are often highly flexible—can become inflexible, stuck, or even stubborn. Here are some suggestions for encouraging flexibility. The first few recommendations primarily focus on modifying the environment for the younger child who has not had practice at developing this skill:

- *Try not to introduce many new things at once.* Reduce the number of "surprises" that your child is exposed to. Provide advance warnings that a change or transition is coming soon. Knowing what to expect will allow your child to get herself into the appropriate frame of mind to handle the situation.

- *Keep to a routine or schedule.* Routines and schedules help a child manage herself throughout the day. As we have already stated, keeping routines loose and allowing for flexibility within them is important, but the basic structure will provide a certain level of stability and comfort for young children.
- *Reduce the complexity of the task.* As we discussed with teaching task initiation, breaking tasks down into smaller parts helps your child avoid feeling overwhelmed. There will be less opportunity for her to "get stuck" and melt down because she doesn't think she can do something.
- *Give your child choices whenever possible.* Children who are relatively inflexible are inclined to show more flexibility when they feel that they have some control over a situation. Having some control also connects with creative children's responsiveness to intrinsic motivation.

As your child gets older, matures, and/or shows more flexibility to the requirements of external contexts, we recommend the following strategies:

- *Support your child through anxiety-provoking situations.* When you can see that your child is clearly anxious about a situation, it is not unreasonable for you to step in and discuss the circumstances with her and even to stay with her until she feels comfortable. For example, perhaps she is overly apprehensive about joining children she doesn't know in a new activity that she'd like to try. Give her time to adjust and get the lay of the land, and then slowly fade away. This will help increase her confidence.
- *Remind your child of her coping toolbox and the strategies she can use if she gets anxious, upset, or if things don't go as planned.* As we discussed with improving emotional self-control, these coping tools can include taking a personal time-out, controlled breathing, and self-talk. They can also include trying to compromise and seeking an adult for assistance.

Do you feel overwhelmed? Please take a deep breath. Okay, now take another one. You are not expected to work on all of the executive planning skills listed in this section or do all of the suggested strategies at once. Instead, select an area of executive functioning that you think your child needs help developing first. Work on that behavior or set of behaviors, and then move on to another when you see some progress. Some of the exercises work to improve more than one skill, making your efforts more efficient.

Parenting Skills for Supporting Your Child's Continued Growth and Development

We want to introduce you to another great resource for improving your child's executive skills—*No Mind Left Behind: Understanding and Fostering Executive Control. The Eight Essential Brain Skills Every Child Needs to Thrive* by licensed psychologist Adam Cox (2007). Similar to Dawson and Guare's *Smart but Scattered,* Dr. Cox's book also identifies key executive skills and offers suggestions to help improve them in your child. Dr. Cox provides a simple and concise list of the types of teaching, or what he calls "surrogate executive control," that can be used to build and enhance the executive planning skills. Here is Dr. Cox's list, with his examples:[80]

1. *Prompting:* "And what do we say when…?"
2. *Reminding:* "Don't forget to look at your…."
3. *Checklists:* "Let's write down everything you need for…."
4. *Preparation*: "In three minutes—that's the time it takes to brush your teeth—we are leaving."
5. *Review*: "Remember what happened last week when you missed dance class? You were really unhappy. Let's not have that happen again. It's time to get ready to leave."
6. *Rehearsal:* "Let's think of some good words to tell Nana you're sorry."
7. *Thinking out loud*: "We'll get our ingredients out now so that…."

8. *Prioritizing:* "We should walk the dog before shopping; otherwise...."

We recommend referring to this list often, as it contains strategies you can use on a daily, if not hourly, or at times minute-by-minute basis with your child. Like Dr. Cox, we have found that using the word *we* when forming plans, reminding, and talking out loud suggests a team approach that increases the possibility of a successful outcome rather than putting your child in a position to be defensive.

Troubleshooting

Developing your child's executive planning skills takes a lot of patience, since change doesn't happen overnight. If after a few weeks you are not seeing improvement in the behaviors you are targeting, ask yourself the following questions:

- *Are my expectations reasonable?* Remember to take into consideration your child's age when gauging what you expect her to be able to do.
- *Have I been consistent in teaching her the skill?* Your child's executive planning skills will only improve with proper (and patient) modeling and instruction.
- *Have I been consistent in following through with the behavior plan?* Your child's skill development is highly dependent upon your consistent follow-through with the necessary structure, routine, supports, celebrations, and consequences to reinforce the new skill.

If you feel like you're not where you'd like to be with your answers to those questions, don't despair. You're new at this, and it takes practice to change behaviors—your child's and your own. Redouble your efforts and keep trying. You'll see progress soon enough. It's not easy, so don't feel discouraged if you aren't seeing the behaviors you'd like to see in your child. When you do see them, you'll feel good for both of you!

"Wide interests? Creative? Distractible? Does my child have ADHD?"

This is a common question that we are asked by parents of creative children. It is normal for creative kids to have some or many of the aforementioned executive planning weaknesses that often go along with ADHD. So how do you know if your child has this disorder?

Are you ready for a profound statement? *A problem is not a problem unless it is a problem.* This means that your child's executive planning weaknesses need to be causing significant problems for him (and you) to be elevated to a level of concern.

Many creative children have executive planning weaknesses, but not all creative children with executive planning weaknesses have Attention Deficit/Hyperactivity Disorder (ADHD). This is defined as having developmentally inappropriate levels of inattention, hyperactivity, and/or impulsivity that occur in two or more settings—home, school, scouts, and/or Little League, to name a few. Teasing apart the difference between executive planning weaknesses and the presence or absence of ADHD in a creative child is quite complex. If you have tried the previous skill-building recommendations consistently without much improvement and your child's executive weaknesses are still causing significant problems, we recommend seeking professional consultation with a child psychologist who is trained in executive functioning deficits/ ADHD and who has experience with creative children. If your child's executive functioning weaknesses are moderate to severe and/or your child has ADHD, professional intervention and support is often necessary to achieve positive results. Nonetheless, all of the strategies discussed in this chapter are completely relevant to a child with ADHD, and we still recommend them to improve your child's executive planning skills.[81]

Boosting Creative Potential and Staying Organized—*or "How to Be Creative and Still Get Things Done!"*

Your creative child is a divergent thinker, and with this "out of the box" thinking often comes weakness in or a lack of the skills of convergence, which are rooted in executive planning skills. These include the ability to manage one's emotions and behaviors by sustaining attention, initiating an action, organizing, planning, prioritizing, and ultimately being self-reflective. While being aware of your own executive planning strengths and challenges, you can improve these skills in your creative child by selecting an area or behavior to target, devising a plan, and consistently supporting your child in carrying it out.

It is important to remember that you need to teach your child a behavior or skill that she does not currently possess, and you need to scaffold and support her abilities as a surrogate to her executive planning skills while they are still developing. Focus on designing a plan that will be successful, as consecutive successes build confidence in your child and motivation for her to tackle the next challenge.

Chapter 11
Essential 21st-Century Skills: Preparing Your Child for the Future

The future ain't what it used to be.

- Yogi Berra

Over the last 15 to 20 years, creativity has been viewed as an "extra" and even to some extent as a form of entertainment, but not a serious part of learning for children in the United States. Yet, a survey in 2009 of more than 400 employers found that their biggest concern was that today's youth lack 21st-century skills that will make them competitive in the job market. Three fourths of those employers viewed creativity and innovation as among the top five skills most important in the current job climate (Fadel, 2011). Fortunately, great thinkers in education, psychology, and neuroscience have come together in a variety of arenas—from edited volumes, national conferences, and TED talks to media specials—to talk about creativity as an essential part of learning and thriving in the 21st century (Robinson, 2006).

The Seven Survival Skills

Just before writing the first version of this book—in 2011, Susan attended the *Learning and the Brain* conference in Boston, which was sponsored by the Harvard Graduate School of Education, the Massachusetts Institute of Technology, the Yale School of Medicine, the University of California at Santa Barbara, and others. This annual conference brings together scholars, researchers, neuroscientists, and practitioners—including teachers, counselors, and educational administrators—to explore a specific theme. The conference theme that year was *Preparing 21st Century Minds: Using Brain Research to Enhance Cognitive Skills for the Future.*

Even though the words *creativity* and *innovation* were not in the conference title, creativity and innovation were front and center in the discussion of how best to move toward optimizing learning and preparing children for life in the 21st century. They were not viewed as "extras" or "nice ideas that we just don't have time for."

There was also quite a buzz at the conference over the contrast between these highly desirable and significantly needed capacities and the way most schools are still teaching in the prolonged aftermath of the No Child Left Behind Act of 2001. Clearly, preparation for a creative and flexible future—a future with many unknowns—is not yet being strongly addressed in our schools. Meanwhile, a number of great minds in education and psychology have come together to predict that a change will be, and in fact *must be*, coming soon.

Tony Wagner (2011), an Innovative Education Fellow at the Technology and Entrepreneurship Center at Harvard and author of *Creating Innovators: The Making of Young People Who Will Change the World*, gave the opening keynote speech. He stated that we need to look to the future—as it evolves—to best prepare our young people to grow and thrive across their lifetimes. He said, "In this new future world, any jobs that can be turned into a routine will be off-shored or automated." Yet, he continued, we are still teaching children in routine ways that prepare them for those sorts of jobs. So to be educating our children in a system of routines, as we do now, is to be educating them for a life that will not be relevant to theirs when they grow up and leave school, moving on to college and to new career pathways. The skills and abilities that our children need at this time are 21st-century skills that will lead to college, career, and optimal engagement as citizens in a global society.

Discussions of 21st-century skills center around "seven survival skills" we need to develop in our students to lead our children through school with passion, motivation, and the ability to move productively forward in life. The seven survival skills for careers, college, and citizenship in the 21st century are the following:

1. Critical thinking and problem solving
2. Collaboration across networks and leading by influence
3. Initiative and entrepreneurship
4. Agility and adaptability
5. Effective oral and written communication
6. Accessing and analyzing information
7. Curiosity and imagination

Each one of these skills is essential to present-day adult careers, but the roots of all of them are developed (or not) early in a child's school career. Let's consider how each of the seven skill sets may be nurtured or squelched in school.

Critical Thinking and Problem Solving

Critical thinking and problem solving relate to the ability to ask the right questions and select the right—or best—problems to pursue. Yet in schools, most questions are asked by teachers, not students, and typically are asked with the expectation of one right answer. Children need to be encouraged to ask and pursue their own open-ended questions, pose their own problems, and sustain interest through meaningful pursuit of learning in areas of interest, passion, and purpose. Rather than one right answer, we need to help children think in terms of how many potential right answers there might be, and what's the *next* right answer?

Take the problem of ocean pollution. Industrial waste and agricultural runoff are polluting rivers and streams, which then send dangerous chemicals into the ocean, and ocean acidification is causing coral reefs to die. How can we help the world's oceans stay clean and healthy? What's the right answer? Since we can't do everything at once, what's the right thing to do for now? And later? Complex problems require complex solutions. We cannot afford to think in terms of one correct answer when it comes to the world's difficult and multifaceted problems. There is no single answer for most problems. What are your child's interests? What are her questions? What problems interest her? What are her ideas for solving those problems?

When a child finds a problem she cares about passionately, intensive research often follows. While it is unlikely that there will be one clear solution that emerges to address the problem, the child will gain deeper understanding and appreciation for multiple possible pathways to improving upon a given problem scenario. Deepened understanding, possible solutions, and further analysis all precede identifying problem solutions.

Collaboration across Networks and Leading by Influence

In 2010, PISA, the Programme for International Assessment, ranked Finland's school systems as the most academically successful internationally. And Finland was listed in the top 10 each year in the decade preceding that assessment. The country's school systems teach using project-based learning and interest-based collaboration. Students who have a common interest within a unit of study work together throughout the unit. This facilitates intrinsic motivation and mutual support and keeps interest high. Those successful schools have implemented the methods that we in the U.S. have generally set aside—whole-child education—which includes interpersonal and intrapersonal reflection, social-emotional development, integrated creative and critical-thinking skills, student choice, intrinsic motivation, and project- and problem-based learning.

These methods are leading Finland's students to maintain engagement, interest, and advanced academic learning while solving real problems.

Collaborative learning projects enrich the learning of all. Productive project-based learning occurs when groups of students gather to study a topic or theme of their choosing and negotiate their roles based on their strengths within the group. Experts consistently document that students who learn collaboratively, choosing a meaningful topic for a project or a problem to solve and working together by using their strengths, learn more than students working alone.

Initiative and Entrepreneurship

Initiative and entrepreneurship are two skills that may be developed in even very young children. As we have mentioned, a number of schools throughout the country are now sponsoring an after-school program called Young Makers Program, in which individuals or teams identify problems and design challenges as catalysts for building inventions. The children engage in problem finding and problem selection, generating potential solutions, prototype design, evaluation, and redesign, along with advertisements and infomercials about the benefits of their work and their product. Responses from mentor-inventors (parents, teachers, and youth leaders), as well as the students themselves, have been overwhelmingly positive, and the programs continue to grow each year and have spread to multiple locations across the country. (See makerfaire.com to find a faire near you.)

However, you don't need to be involved in a structured program to help your child learn initiative and entrepreneurship. Entrepreneurship throughout the ages often has begun on a kitchen table, in an art space, in a wood shop, or in the garage. Dozens of books are available on the invention and patenting process for children, as well as for the larger do-it-yourself (DIY) movement. Scores of Internet sites have arisen in the past few years to aid artisans and inventors in marketing their wares. Perhaps the best-known and most frequented is Etsy. Etsy.com bills itself as the world's most vibrant handmade marketplace. The structure is in place for people to set up their own web page under the larger Etsy site to share their inventions, art, or designs with potential buyers worldwide. This is a great way for children to feel motivate to create a product that they can then offer to others, and the sale of that product can provide validation for their energy and efforts.

Agility and Adaptability

Agility and adaptability are essential for our times. Every day we are presented with new local and global problems and challenges, along with shifting cultural, environmental, and social climates; yet this is in stark contrast to the regularity and conformity of our schools. Mind you, students—children of all ages—need some regularity, some consistency, some dependability. However, rigidity in curriculum, teaching methods, and learning environments will not prepare children for the rapidly changing world in which we live. As we have discussed at length, flexibility is central to the creative process; it is a key aspect of divergent thinking. Flexibility is a skill that can be taught and nurtured in our children as we support them in developing mental agility and adaptability.

Teachers can incorporate flexibility in their classrooms though differentiated instruction, in which there are choices and options for the content, processes, and products that students engage in and produce during a course of study. For example, in studying Medieval Europe, students might study the culture and customs, the key political trends, or the artistic and scientific advances of the time. For products, students may be given choice based on their interests and talents, including such options as writing a first-person narrative about life as a Medieval serf, creating a video, performing a play, designing a multimedia presentation, or producing a standard report. Grading may be adjusted according to the requirements of each assignment, thereby providing another form of flexibility relevant to the differentiation process.

We need to make sure that our children progress through school learning not just to read text and write reports about what they read, but also to think about topics from a variety of contexts and perspectives and to create complex and multilevel projects that demonstrate their knowledge and offer creative ways of expressing it.

Effective Oral and Written Communication

While on the one hand we want our students to be able to move beyond writing a standard report about the latest unit in class, we also want them to be able to actually write that report if they need to—and to do so well. Effective oral and written communication goes well beyond the ability to write the standard five-paragraph essay. It is clearly evident that our students are not developing true literacy: the connections of reading, writing, and speaking. Literature today is offered in bite-sized chunks, and most students are not given the opportunity to read books of a quality and at a level that will expose them to different times, places, and viewpoints. In addition, students lack the ability to write formally, to write and speak with their own voice. Fluency in verbal expression and the ability to express oneself through various modes and media—including digital storytelling, video production, website design, wikis—are part of the new literacy needed for communication and collaboration in the 21st-century global society.

Accessing and Analyzing Information

There has been a significant shift in teaching and learning over the last decade or so in terms of how we access information. It used to be that we relied on teachers and textbooks to deliver what our students needed to know, and maybe a good encyclopedia. But now information on virtually any topic may be accessed electronically by anyone. In essence, information has been democratized. However, the glut of information now available makes it more important than ever to teach children skills of analysis, evaluation, synthesis, and application of information to relevant learning projects. Enabling children to formulate their questions, research and access needed information, and devise effective means to express their learning goes back to project-based learning. This is not a new approach, but it is an approach that is attaining renewal, and constitutes a renaissance in teaching and learning, as the Knowledge Age of the last century moves into what some are calling the Innovation Age.

Curiosity and Imagination

We've discussed the concepts of curiosity and imagination in some depth earlier in the book, and it should be no surprise that they are among the seven survival skills that we want to encourage and enhance in our children so that they will become the problem solvers of tomorrow. Curiosity involves wondering about how things are, how they got to be that way, and how they could be different. Curious thinkers explore questions and possibilities that are grounded in what they know and that extend to the realm of the possible. Curious children ask questions, seemingly constantly, about how and why things are the way they are. Why is the sky blue? How are the skyscrapers built? What holds up clouds? What happens after we die? Why are their different religions? How did they get those big stones set up at Stonehenge or for the pyramids in Egypt?

Curiosity also can take the form of "what if" possibilities. What if we made plastic utensils out of another material? How about corn or some other natural substance? Could they be biodegradable? What if a law was passed that people were required to live within 25 miles of where they worked? Would this lower pollution? What if students could spend half the day studying anything that interested them? Would they be motivated to learn more, or would they be lazy and do minimal work?

"What if" questions lead thinking from what is into the realm of what might be—the realm of the imaginative. Children use their imaginations in this way to ponder things that have yet to be thought, made, or done. One driving motivation behind imagination is a desire for the images and the ideas for inventions or concepts that don't yet exist. Imagination takes us from what is to what might be, a key aspect of problem solving and creativity.[86]

Learning for Life in Our Times

Bernie Trilling and Charles Fadel, authors of *21st Century Skills: Learning for Life in Our Times* (2009), speak frequently at conferences and expand notions of how to go about teaching with and for creativity. Both were founding board members of the Partnership for 21st Century Skills, an institute that focused on developing new skills for grades K-12. They are both dedicated to integrating creativity and problem solving within our current school curriculums.

What began as the Partnership for 21st Century Skills (P21) has become Battelle for Kids (BFK)—a national nonprofit organization that advocates for 21st-century readiness for all students. BFK provides tools and resources to help the American education system find ways to compete in a global economy where innovation is essential. It does so by fusing the traditional curriculum of reading, writing, and arithmetic (the three Rs) with the four Cs of critical thinking and problem-solving, communication, collaboration, and creativity and innovation. Although leading school districts are already doing this, BFK's goal is to get local, state, and federal policies put into place that support this approach for every school.

In Trilling and Fadel's book, they emphasize the deep and powerful learning that takes place when creativity, learning and innovation skills, and collaboration are explicitly taught and modeled in meaningful contexts, as well as applied to real-world problems and projects. They also underscore the importance of applied creativity—the bridge from individual creativity to creative collaboration and a creative product. The authors elaborate on the aspects of creativity that students must learn throughout their school years in order to cultivate their own innate creativity, learn the skills of creative collaboration, and plan for follow-through with meaningful applications within the contexts of various projects and settings.

Examples of creative projects that integrate topics and that are applicable to the here and now abound. At King Middle School in Maine, students learn about soil bacteria by conducting investigations and creating multimedia pamphlets. They interview professional microbiologists and cartoonists, and after designing their informational pamphlets, they distribute them to local garden centers, university departments, and florists. In San Diego, High Tech High School biology students use DNA barcoding to develop forensic techniques that may be used to help African wildlife by working collaboratively with wildlife protection officials in the U.S. and Africa. At Ferryway School in Massachusetts, fifth graders explore history, science, technology, and engineering by designing their own waterwheels. Then they visit Saugus Iron Works, originated in the 1640s, to see the original designs and constructions of these devices. These projects range from exploratory and informational to creative and innovative.

This is a good point at which to stop for a moment and consider the nuances between the terms *creativity* and *innovation*. These two concepts are often linked, yet there is a difference between them. The word *creativity* refers primarily to originality of thinking. In contrast, *innovation* is the creation of improved or more effective products, processes, services, technologies, or ideas that are utilized or applied in communities, businesses, and society. Innovation refers more directly to the construction and use of an invention or the application of a creative method in a broader and more generalized sense, such as when applied to a workplace, community, or society at large. Increasingly, the skills involved in innovation are being recognized as those that separate students who are prepared for more complex life and work environments in the 21st century from those who are not.

Working Creatively with Others

Most innovative advances in our world today involve collaboration. Adults need specific skills in order to collaborate with others to bring their creative ideas to fruition. Working creatively with others depends on strong interpersonal skills and includes the ability to:[89]

- ❍ Develop, implement, and communicate new ideas to others effectively
- ❍ Be open and responsive to new and diverse perspectives
- ❍ Incorporate group input and feedback into the work
- ❍ Demonstrate originality and inventiveness and understand the real-world limits to adopting new ideas
- ❍ View failure as opportunities to learn
- ❍ Understand that creativity and innovation is a long-term, cyclical process of small successes and frequent mistakes
- ❍ Act on creative ideas to make a tangible and useful contribution

Children can learn these skills if we teach them, and experts like Trilling and Fadel argue that the classroom is as good a place as any. We argue that the home is too. We can—and we should—help our children develop these abilities so that they can use their creative ideas to develop innovative products and solutions to the complex problems of today—and tomorrow.

Boosting Creative Potential—Now and Into the Future

You may be seeing a connection between what you have read about nurturing your child's development and preparing her for a successful future in the modern world. The seven survival skills discussed in this chapter are explained in terms of learning, but not necessarily learning in school. Many, if not most, of the seven skills involve aspects of creativity—solving complex problems (divergent thinking), finding ways to access resources (collaboration), agility and adaptability (flexibility), entrepreneurship (risk taking), and of course, curiosity and imagination.

So how are those qualities both relevant and related? Well, first, and a key point of this book, is that regardless of what your child's school is or is not doing to prepare your child for the 21st century, *you* can play a significant, positive role in nurturing the seven survival skills at home and in out-of-home enrichment activities. In fact, that's what this book is about! So by reading and following some of our suggestions, not only are you helping your child to create and to follow her own passions and interests in satisfying and productive ways, you also will be preparing her for success in our rapidly changing world.

Raising a creative child is embarking on and committing to "the road less traveled." It involves purposeful parenting that emphasizes your child's exploring, searching, experimenting, daydreaming, wondering, improvising, questioning, and debating everything from why she should brush her teeth even though she is going to be growing adult teeth soon to wondering how to reduce the amount of stray animals in the neighborhood. Parenting a creative child requires patience, open-mindedness, respect, and trust in your child's ideas. It involves understanding that development and maturity take time and that it is our job as parents to provide our children with the space to grow and make mistakes while also setting boundaries to keep them safe. Most importantly, effective parenting enriches the life of your child in the present and for the future and supports her in attaining a meaningful and fulfilling life. And guess what? Despite the fatigue you may experience from time to time, boosting creativity in your child's life will enhance and give meaning to your life, too. We wish you the best on your journey, wherever it—and your child—may take you.

References and Resources

Amabile, T. (1989). *Growing up creative: Nurturing a lifetime of creativity.* New York: Crown.

Benke, K. (2010). *Rip the page! Adventures in creative writing.* Boston: Trumpeter Books.

Bronson, P., & Merryman, A. (2009). *Nurture shock: New thinking about children.* New York: Hachette.

Bronson, P., & Merryman, A. (2010). *The creativity crisis: For the first time, research shows that American creativity is declining. What went wrong—and how can we fix it.* Retrieved from www.thedailybeast.com/newsweek/2010/07/10/the-creativity-crisis.print.html

Brown, S. (2008). *Stuart Brown: Play is more than fun.* Retrieved from www.ted.com/talks/stuart_brown_says_play_is_more_than_fun_it_s_vital.html

Caffrey, J. W. (2011). *Nurturing brilliance: Discovering and developing your child's gifts.* Scottsdale, AZ: Great Potential Press.

Cox, A. (2007). *No mind left behind: Understanding and fostering executive control. The eight essential brain skills every child needs to thrive.* New York: Penguin.

Crawford, L., & Fox, S. (2007). *City walks with kids: San Francisco: 50 adventures on foot.* San Francisco: Chronicle Books.

Csikszentmihalyi, M. (1997). *Creativity: Flow and the psychology of discovery and invention.* New York: Basic Books.

Dacey, J., & Packer, A. (1992). *The nurturing parent: How to raise creative, loving, responsible children.* New York: Fireside.

Daniels, S., & Piechowski, M. M. (2009). *Living with intensity.* Scottsdale, AZ: Great Potential Press.

Davis, G. A. (2004). *Creativity is forever* (5th ed.). Dubuque, IA: Kendall/ Hunt.

Dawson, P., & Guare, R. (2009). *Smart but scattered.* New York: Guilford Press.

Dweck, C. (2008). *Mindset: The new psychology of success. How we can learn to fulfill our potential.* New York: Ballantine.

Eckhoff, A., & Urback, J. (2008). Understanding imaginative thinking during childhood: Sociocultural conceptions of creativity and imaginative thought. *Journal of Early Childhood Education, 36*, 179-185.

Emberly, E. (2006). *Make a world.* New York: Little, Brown, & Co.

Ericsson, K. A. (2006). The influence of experience and deliberate practice on the development of superior expert performance. In K. A. Ericsson, N. Charness, P. Feltovich, & R. R. Hoffman (Eds.), *Cambridge handbook of expertise and expert performance* (pp. 685706). Cambridge, UK: Cambridge University Press.

Fadel, C. K. (2011). *21st-century skills: The imperative for teaching creativity and innovation in the schools.* Keynote address at the Learning and the Brain conference, Preparing 21st-Century Minds: Using Brain Research to Enhance Cognitive Skills for the Future, Boston.

Goertzel, V., Goertzel, M. G., Goertzel, T. G., & Hansen, A. M. W. (2004). *Cradles of eminence: Childhoods of more than four hundred famous men and women* (2nd ed.). Scottsdale, AZ: Great Potential Press.

Goleman, D., Kaufman, P., & Ray, M. (1992). *The creative spirit.* New York: Plume.

Greene, R. (2010). *The explosive child: A new approach for understanding and parenting frustrating and "chronically inflexible" children.* New York: Harper.

Hallissy, J. (2010). *The write start: A guide to nurturing writing at every stage, from scribbling to forming letters and writing stories.* Boston: Trumpeter Books.

Kaufman, J. C., & Beghetto, R. A. (2009). Beyond big and little: The Four C Model of creativity. *Review of General Psychology, 13*(1), 1-12.

Lee, D. (2011). *Biomimicry: Inventions inspired by nature.* Tonawanda, NY: Kids Can Press.

Leimbach, J., & Vydra, J. (2005). *Primarily creativity.* Waco, TX: Prufrock Press.

Louv, R. (2005). *Last child in the woods: Saving our children from nature-deficit disorder.* Chapel Hill, NC : Algonquin Books.

Lovecky, D. V. (2004). *Different minds: Gifted children with AD/HD, Asperger Syndrome, and other learning deficits.* Philadelphia: Jessica Kingsley.

Mayesky, M. (2009). *Creative activities for young children* (9th ed.). Clifton Park, NY: Delmar Cengage Learning.

Palladino, L. (1999). *Dreamers, discovers, and dynamos: How to help the child who is bright, bored, and having problems in school.* New York: Random House.

Piechowski, M. M. (2006). *"Mellow out," they say. If I only could: Intensities and sensitivities of the young and bright.* Madison, WI: Yunasa Books.

Piirto, J. (2004). *Understanding creativity.* Scottsdale, AZ: Great Potential Press.

Pink, D. (2006). *A whole new mind: Why right-brainers will rule the future.* New York: Riverhead Books.

Reznick, C. (2009). *The power of your child's imagination: How to transform stress and anxiety into joy and success.* New York: Perigree.

Richards, R. (Ed.). (2007). *Everyday creativity and new views of human nature: Psychological, social, and spiritual perspectives.* Washington, DC: American Psychological Association.

Rivero, L. (2010). *A parent's guide to gifted teens: Living with intense and creative adolescents.* Scottsdale, AZ: Great Potential Press.

Robinson, K. (2006). *Ken Robinson says schools kill creativity.* Retrieved from www.ted.com/talks/ken_robinson_says_schools_kill_creativity.html

Ruef, K. (2003). *The private eye: (5X) looking/thinking by analogy.* Lyle, WA: The Private Eye Project.

Runco, M. (2011). *Innovative teaching: Implications of creativity research for the classroom.* Presented at the Learning & the Brain conference "Preparing 21st Century Minds: Using Brain Research to Enhance Cognitive Skills for the Future," Boston.

Salmi, N. (Ed.). (2009). Frommer's San Francisco with kids. Hoboken, NJ: Wiley.

Singer, J. (1999). Imagination. In M. A. Runco & S. R. Pritzker (Eds.), *Encyclopedia of creativity* (pp. 13-25). London: Academic Press.

Sonheim, C. (2010). *Drawing lab for mixed-media artists: 52 creative exercises to make drawing fun.* Beverly, MA: Quarry Books.

Torrance, E. P. (n.d.). *Figural Torrance Tests of Creative Thinking (TTCT): Thinking creatively with pictures. Bensenville, IL: Scholastic Testing Service.*

Treffinger, D. J. (2000). *Practice problems for creative problem solving* (3rd ed.). Waco, TX: Prufrock Press.

Trilling, B., & Fadel, C. (2009). *21st century skills: Learning for life in our times.* San Francisco: John Wiley & Sons.

Wagner, T. (2011). *Learning to innovate, innovating to learn.* Retrieved from www.slideshare.net/globaleducationforum/learning-to- innovate-innovating-to-learn-madrid-keynote-10-11tony-wagner

Wagner, T. (2012). *Creating innovators: The making of young people who will change the world.* New York: Scribner.

Wallas, G. (1926). *The art of thought.* New York: Harcourt.

Webb, J. T., Amend, E. R., Webb, N. E., Goerss, J., Beljan, P., & Olenchak, F. R. (2005). *Misdiagnosis and dual diagnoses of gifted children and adults: ADHD, bipolar, OCD, Asperger's, depression, and other disorders.* Tucson, AZ: Great Potential Press.

Westberg, K. L. (1996). The effects of teaching students how to invent. *Journal of Creative Behavior, (30)*, 249-267.

Willis, J. A. (2009). *Inspiring middle school minds: Gifted, creative, and challenging.* Scottsdale, AZ: Great Potential Press.

Wolfe, P. (2010). *Brain matters: Translating research into classroom practice.* Alexandria, VA: ASCD.

Note: The following are from the text box by Nicole Tretault in Chapter 1.

Roger E. Beaty, et al. "Robust prediction of individual creative ability from brain functional connectivity." *Proceedings of the National Academy of Sciences of the United States of America* vol. 115,5 (2018): 1087-1092. doi:10.1073/pnas.1713532115

Catherine Best et al., "The Relationship Between Subthreshold Autistic Traits, Ambiguous Figure Perception and Divergent Thinking," *J Autism Dev Disord* 45, no. 12 (Dec 2015), https://doi.org/10.1007/s10803-015-2518-2.

White, Holly A., and Priti Shah. "Uninhibited Imaginations: Creativity in Adults with Attention-Deficit/Hyperactivity Disorder." *Personality and Individual Differences* 40, no. 6 (2006/04/01/ 2006): 1121-31. https://doi.org/https://doi.org/10.1016/j.paid.2005.11.007. http://www.sciencedirect.com/science/article/pii/S0191886905003764.

Chunshui Yu, et al. "White matter tract integrity and intelligence in patients with mental retardation and healthy adults." *NeuroImage* vol. 40,4 (2008): 1533-41. doi:10.1016/j.neuroimage.2008.01.063

About the Authors

Susan Daniels, Ph.D., is an educational psychologist, professor, author, and Co-founder of the Summit Center, specializing in the assessment of and psychological service for gifted, creative, and twice exceptional youth.

As co-founder, with Dr. Dan Peters, of the Summit Center, Dr. Daniels has provided personality, learning, and creativity assessments for children and adolescents as part of the Summit Center's neuropsychological and psychoeducational assessments of youth. Susan also serves as a creativity coach with adolescents and adults and as a youth life coach. As a creativity coach, Susan works one-to-one with individuals to develop an understanding of, and skills to help develop, their personal creative potential. As life coach, Susan supports and encourages young people and adults in identifying personal strengths, navigating life challenges, celebrating creativity, and designing a vision for a best possible life. Susan is most interested in personal creativity —also referred to as everyday creativity—that creativity that we can tap into and develop to both improve and enrich our lives.

Dr. Daniels is an internationally recognized expert in the fields of gifted education and creativity, with numerous publications and presentations given annually at educational and psychological conferences. She specializes in the social and emotional development of gifted, creative, and 2e children and adolescents, the intensity and sensitivity of gifted individuals across the lifespan, visual learning and teaching, and the development of creative potential. Formerly,

Susan was Professor of Educational Psychology and Counseling at California State University—San Bernardino, for twenty years, where she directed the Graduate Certificate in Gifted Education and taught courses in child and adolescent development; gifted education; and creativity, thinking, and problem solving. Dr. Daniels is author of *Visual Learning and Teaching: An Essential Guide for Educators K-8*. She is also co-editor and co-author of *Living with Intensity.*

Daniel B. Peters, Ph.D., is a psychologist, author, co-founder and Executive Director of the Summit Center. Dr. Peters has devoted his career to the assessment and treatment of children, adolescents, and families, specializing in overcoming worry and fear, learning differences such as dyslexia, and issues related to giftedness and twice-exceptionality.

Dr. Dan is the author of *Make Your Worrier a Warrior: A Guide to Conquering Your Child's Fears*, its companion children's book *From Worrier to Warrior*, and the *Warrior Workbook*. He is host of the "Parent Footprint Podcast with Dr. Dan".

Dr. Dan speaks regularly at national conferences and to the media, as well as writes articles, on a variety of topics including parenting, learning differences, special needs, family, education and more. He serves on the Editorial Board for the 2e News, the Executive Board for the 2e Center for Research and Professional Development at Bridges Academy, and as Co-Chair of the NAGC's Assessments of Giftedness Special Interest Group, and advisory board for Gifted Research and Outreach (GRO).

Dr. Peters was recognized as "2018 SENG Mental Health Professional of the Year" by Supporting Emotional Needs of Gifted, and as "2016 Allen Ewig Champion for Children" by Aldea Children and Family Services. He also received the 2013 CAG Distinguished Service Award from the California Association for Gifted.

CPSIA information can be obtained
at www.ICGtesting.com
Printed in the USA
BVHW091829300722
643341BV00006B/15